STEVE PREDA  GREGORY CLEARY

PINNACLE

FIVE
PRINCIPLES THAT
TAKE YOUR BUSINESS
TO THE TOP OF THE MOUNTAIN

ISBN: 978-0-9984478-8-9 (hardcover)
ISBN: 978-0-9984478-9-6 (paperback)
ISBN: 979-8-9860636-0-7 (e-book)
ISBN: 979-8-9860636-1-4 (audio book)

Amershire Publishing, Glen Allen, Virginia

Printed in the United States of America

Cover Design: Jason Anscomb

Text Design and Illustrations: Andy Meaden, Zoltan Ember, Will Sargent, and Greg Kimmes

Editing and Proofreading: Christina Palaia, Nicole Hall, and Barry Lyons

Indexing: Toni Culley

Dedication by Steve:

To my beloved children: Emilia, Paula, Istvan, and Sandor.
You make it all worthwhile!

Dedication by Greg:

To my amazing soul mate and bride, Julie who has stood by my side as I
traveled on this journey without ever once complaining.
My son Benjamin and daughter Samantha, who have turned out to be
amazing people that make us proud every day.
My heart is full of love because of you.

Contents

Preface

By Gregory Cleary

Do you want to be in a category of one in your industry?

We want to help you grow faster than you ever thought possible. We want to start a revolution for entrepreneurs who create all the jobs, careers, innovation, and value.

Pinnacle is an evolution of everything I have learned. My journey to here started in 1985 selling and teaching the Brian Tracy curriculum. Brian had created the Phoenix Seminar. It was all about self-improvement, goal-setting, communication, relationships, and health. I taught the class hundreds of times to thousands of people.

That was the start of my journey that led me to be the National Sales Manager for Peak Performers Network, Co-Founder of Team Trac, and Founder of Action Learning Corporation. Then in 2010, I became a Certified Entrepreneurial Operating System (EOS) Implementer. I was in on the ground floor with EOS and was the eighth Certified EOS Implementer in the world.

I spent almost a decade implementing EOS for 149 companies and conducting over one thousand documented sessions. Upon my departure from the EOS community in fall of 2019, I was ranked #1 in the world for number of sessions conducted annually and revenue generated. I had become the first EOS Implementer to earn over a million dollars in annual fees. I quickly went on to break my own records by setting new records.

My epiphany, and why you should care?:

The reason I was so successful is that I have *always* focused on my clients, their experience during our journey, and delivering results. Every company on the planet is unique, including yours. Even companies in the same industry, in the same market, selling the same products are unique.

Therefore, "One Size Fits All" is a terrible approach to developing your business operating system. As I look back over my career working with dozens of well-known speakers and authors, I've concluded that nobody has the market cornered on good ideas or business tools. Want proof? Just open your smartphone or desktop and count how many applications you rely on.

Pinnacle Business Guides wants to help you create your very own personal business operating system for your unique company. No two companies are the same, so no two business operating systems will be the same.

Here's the formula for developing your unique business operating system:

People + Purpose + Playbooks + Perform = Profit

Pinnacle is an evolution. We've packed up some of the finest business tools on the planet—curated and refined from hundreds of time-tested books, proven tools, and concepts, which can be customized for your unique climb.

Steve and I are standing on the shoulders of the 100+ Pinnacle Business Guides who are out there teaching, learning, and evolving with every session to help their clients grow! It's not an easy journey, but in the end the view is incredible.

Let's Climb!

Gregory Cleary

Naples, Florida, March 20, 2022

INTRODUCTION: BEFORE THE CLIMB

The Pinnacle

Medium-term Milestones

Annual Summit

Quarterly Lookout

Basecamp

*"Each system is perfectly designed to give you
exactly what you are getting today."*

—W. Edwards Deming

Do you own a small business with more than a handful of employees? Are you frustrated that your business has flatlined? Do you feel drained by working long hours and only dreaming of having an energized team ready to step up and lead? Do you nurse an ambition to scale your business into one that dominates its niche? Are you concerned that time is *running out* and you may never fulfill your dreams?

If you answered yes to any of the above, you are holding the right book.

You have acquired or built a privately held business. You know how to get and serve customers, and you have grown to withstand the pressure of meeting payroll and surviving challenging times. Your business has prevailed and even grown over the years, and you believe that with perseverance you can keep going indefinitely. In one word, you are an entrepreneur.

Sadly, not all entrepreneurs create successful businesses. Most fail. To succeed in business, you need business-building skills too. Entrepreneurship is about both risk-taking and business building.

Look at somebody who is fit: they have a system. Look at somebody who has a great marriage: they have a system. Look at somebody who has great kids: they have a system. Success leaves clues to how all the great business mountains have been climbed.

So, is there a system that enables you as an entrepreneurial risk-taker to acquire the business skills and structure you need to play bigger and dramatically grow your small businesses without getting an MBA?

Welcome to the Pinnacle journey!

Your journey is going to be unique, and we will show you the Principles and the Practices that you will need to climb to the top of your own business mountain.

We have created a formula that applies to any company and is customizable for your business. We believe that there are five things you need to obsess about as an entrepreneurial leader. These are: People, Purpose, Playbooks, Perform, and Profit.

We have broken these principles down to fifteen practices that help you clarify and implement the five Pinnacle Principles in your business.

What you will get is a personalized operating system that brings you the strategy that differentiates you from your competition. Your operating system will allow you to execute your vision and your plan so that you can have the business you want to make the impact you want, and to make the world a better place.

This book contains all the information you need, but it cannot convey one thing: experience. To acquire the experience, you need a guide who will help you build that personalized operating system for your business by bringing you the right tools at the right time to maximize the five Pinnacle Principles for the exact stage of development of your business.

By focusing on the five Pinnacle Principles and applying the fifteen Pinnacle Practices explained in this book, you will learn:

- What it takes to finally feel successful and acquire the momentum of growth that you've dreamed about

- How to make your business a category of one in your industry

- How to build an energized team of fellow leaders who share your vision and are determined to realize it

- How to 5X the value of your business in the next five years (for example, by growing your revenues 2.5-times while doubling your profit margin)

- How to create more time in your business for doing what you are excited about doing

- How to implement tools that will allow you to be more present with your family and support them in all the ways you've always wished for, and

- What it takes to create options for yourself so that you can begin to live your ideal life inside or outside your current business.

The Pinnacle Model

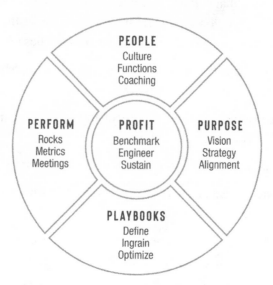

Your Pinnacle journey starts with the **PEOPLE** principle, where you first define your **Culture** to attract and promote the right people for your organization. Then you determine the **Functions** your business needs right now, and we'll assess your talent pool to identify the people that need your **Coaching** to realize their potential.

Next, we consider the **PURPOSE** principle and paint a compelling **Vision** for your organization and to to figure out the right **Strategy** that will get you there. No one builds a great company alone, and therefore you must create **Alignment** around your Vision and Strategy to get all your people rowing in the same direction.

As soon as your Vision is clear and your team is moving toward it with a Strategy that everyone understands and is able to execute, it is time to **Define** your critical **PLAYBOOKS** and **Ingrain** them as habits throughout your business. Thereafter, your job becomes to **Optimize** your Playbooks and create a cycle of continuous improvement.

From there, your next stop is the **PERFORM** principle, which will help you establish a well-oiled machine of execution. Your people will start holding each other accountable to implementing your plans through setting annual goals and quarterly **Rocks**, and measuring their progress using weekly **Metrics** and tackling important topics in productive **Meetings**.

At that point, you turn your attention to the **PROFIT** principle. It's time for you to **Benchmark** your company against the elite of your industry, and **Engineer** your business to achieve best-in-class profitability and **Sustain** it indefinitely.

You will then map out your climb to the Pinnacle of your business. Will you try to make this journey yourself, or seek out a guide? If the latter, how do you choose the right one for your business?

Finally, you will see what life looks like from the Pinnacle. What are your opportunities upon arrival? Only from the top is the next higher peak visible.

This is not a start-up manual and does not review the fundamentals of building a business from scratch. Instead, think of this book more like a map with a list of directions and mile markers. To that, add the road warrior experience you already have to make your business rise to the pinnacle of success.

Pinnacle gives you a framework and explains the five Principles and fifteeen Practices that will help turn your viable small business into a dynamically growing, category-defining, and highly profitable enterprise. It tells you how to increase the value—by five times—of your already sustainable business over the next five years.

A word of warning!

If you are a solopreneur or running a mom-and-pop venture that is struggling to get through most days, stop reading and get your feet under you first.

Likewise, if your goal is to create or maintain a lifestyle business, one that provides a decent income and maintains a success level where you retain decision-making power indefinitely, you won't find this book necessary.

This guidebook is for growers: ambitious business owners who want to create an extraordinary, self-managing, and highly valuable entity that they ultimately are willing to allow to grow up and release into the world.

If you are ready to create an exceptional growth business with an amazing team and to quintuple its value in the next five years, this is the book for you. It distills thirty years of studying the business classics and our work with over five hundred businesses into a step-by-step manual you can use to take your business to the top of the mountain.

Let's begin your journey to the Pinnacle!

BASE CAMP

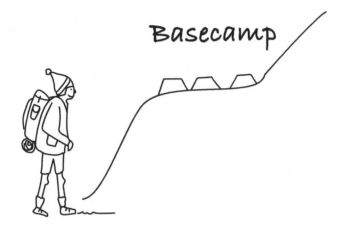

Basecamp

"Because in the end, you won't remember the time you spent in an office or mowing your lawn. Climb that damn mountain."

—Jack Kerouac

WHY 5X YOUR PRIVATE BUSINESS?

"Anything unusual that you can produce has quadruple, quintuple the value, precisely because your opponent is likely to do the predictable stuff."

—Viswanathan Anand

Steve met with him around 2005, when Antal was a fledgling business owner running an automotive tool machining shop in western Hungary. He had worked for automakers such as Mercedes, BMW, and Audi in Germany before starting up his own machining shop.

Back then, Antal was what Michael Gerber, author of *The E-Myth Revisited,* would call a "technician" rather than an "entrepreneur." He was an expert at fabricating steel structures that enabled the German automakers to procure injection-molded plastic parts for their cars, such as engine parts and dashboard switches. Over time he hired helpers and learned to build a team. His business grew from $16 million in revenue to over $27 million over a ten-year period, representing a modest 6.2 percent annual growth rate. However, the business grew its cash profits at a higher rate, attracted a higher valuation multiple, and paid off debt. As a result, its equity value more than tripled over that time period from $15 million to over $51 million.

Actually, Antal's experience is a rather ordinary story; we've seen businesses grow substantially faster. Private equity investors look to *triple* the value of their investee companies over three years, which can be achieved by *doubling* a company's revenue and growing its profit margin by 50 percent in that time period.

On a five-year time horizon, an ordinary private business can feasibly grow its revenues by 2.5 times, by growing 20 percent a year. Such growth necessitates and forces internal process improvements and external differentiation, which can double net profit margin, resulting in a 5X or higher growth in the value of the business.

Achieving a 20 percent year over year growth rate can be achieved with a combination of procuring new business sales, increasing the value and price of your offerings, and cross-selling other products and services to your customers.

Doubling profit margins in five years can be accomplished by differentiating your services through increasing market focus, branding, and defining a clear strategy that your people understand and can execute.

Another way to double your profit margin is to systemize your business, which will create consistency and improve cost-efficiency and help control expenses further through delegation to lower-cost resources. As a byproduct of systemization, the quality of your products will also improve, enabling you to charge still higher prices.

These are just examples and there are other approaches to 5X-ing the value of your business. One of the easiest is to pay off debt. Another one is to find strategic partners who will get you into new distribution channels. Just by growing your company, your valuation multiple will expand as well, enhancing the worth of the business more than the increase in its profits.

Do you find this growth target ambitious? In the following pages we will prove to you that generating these numbers is entirely feasible and likely even a conservative expectation. Since Steve started coaching leadership teams five years ago, his clients have on average grown their top lines by over 20 percent per annum and have achieved more than 50 percent average annual growth in profits. Gregory's results have been similar and span over a decade.

Back in the early 2010s, a client of Steve's investment banking business, a bottler of nonalcoholic beverages, grew its revenue by 36 percent and its profit margin from 21 percent to 25 percent over an eighteen-month period when Steve's investment banking team was preparing it for sale to a private equity group. These improvements were generated by a cross-selling campaign, launching a couple of new products, and cost engineering. These top- and bottom-line growths were achieved without any management or operational improvements to the business, which could have added substantial further growth.

We will show you how, by following the five Pinnacle Principles of People, Purpose, Playbooks, Perform, and Profit, your business can become an unstoppable organization with a great culture, empowered leaders, and employees who are on a mission to achieve your vision by executing a differentiated strategy for your business.

We will explain how to create a structure of peer accountability that will allow you to attract A-Players: employees who love your culture and consistently perform at a high level. A-Players hold each other accountable for reaching financial targets and development goals that they co-create with you using basic Pinnacle tools such as FAST Rocks, Win-the-Week Scoreboards, and Meeting Structures.

Together in this book, we will build a Strategic Vision and Execution Plan for your business and improve your strategic positioning and differentiation using the Strategy Squares framework.

We will then teach you how to create Playbooks that will allow you to establish consistency and scalability and foster delegation and growth in your business. You will define and ingrain these systems and learn to consider lean principles and intelligent automation to continually improve upon them.

Finally, we will benchmark your profitability to your industry's leaders and engineer your business to match, sustain, and possibly even surpass that ratio over time.

So, why set an ambitious 5X growth target for the next five years?

Broadly speaking, growing the value of your small business by a factor of five is a worthwhile, energizing, and achievable goal. It will give you the freedom, financial independence, and sense of achievement so that you can become all you can be in life, with or without your business.

But there are also very specific reasons why you must 5X your small business. Firstly, conservative goals don't move people. If you want to attract A-Players, you need to broadcast an ambitious plan that they will find worth working toward. After all, who is excited by a single-digit percent growth plan?

Secondly, your goal should be to create the leading company in your niche. That means growing faster than your competitors. Show me an A-Player who does not want to work for—and thus be—the best in their field!

Thirdly, you will start creating your "ideal life" as soon as possible.

We assume that reading this book you already own a maturing business, defined as generating at least $2 million in revenue and having 10 full-time equivalent employees with a minimum of 10 percent owner's discretionary earnings or profit. That business would represent a minimum company value of $600,000 to $1 million.

5X-ing that business, even one valued at the low end of that spectrum, would create an at least $3 million to $5 million nest egg. That's enough for most people to start living their ideal life. (See more about how to get there in Steve's earlier book: *Buyable: Your Guide to Building a Self-Managing, Fast-Growing, and High-Profit Business.*)

One of our coaching clients, the real estate brokerage and property management company Reichle Klein Group (RKG), accelerated its growth by deploying two business management blueprints. CEO Harlan Reichle first implemented the Entrepreneurial Operating System and later decided to go to the next level and master the Pinnacle Principles.

RKG's nascent property management business doubled in size, and its profitability multiplied when the business clarified its vision and strategy, empowered a leadership team, and started replacing B-Players with A-Players.

Harlan was able to step back from day-to-day operations and free himself up to focus on strategic relationships and spend more time with his wife, on charitable activities, and wild game hunting.

Using a custom operating system such as Pinnacle allows you to start the process at the point you have already reached. Instead of following a cookie-cutter recipe, you take a full physical assessment and start by fixing the issues that give you the most improvement at the lowest cost of time and money.

You then gradually move up from there, using Pinnacle climbing tools as and when they best help you, curated by your Pinnacle Business Guide. Read on to discover many of these tools on the pages of this book.

Key Ideas from Why 5X Your Private Business

- Set out to quintuple your business in five years. This process will generate excitement and challenge you to reinvent your business and make it a leader in your niche.

- Achieving 5X is feasible without acquisitions through increasing sales by 20 percent per year for five years, while doubling your net profit margin through differentiating, increasing strategic focus, and systemizing your business.

- The Pinnacle Principles work for already maturing businesses generating $2 million or more in annual sales and having at least 10 full-time permanent employees.

- Following the Pinnacle Principles is a way for you to transition to living your ideal life or at least creating a business with the potential to get you to it, in the foreseeable future.

But before we talk about the five Pinnacle Principles, let's first discuss in the next chapter whether you should consider embarking on this type of journey in the first place.

ARE YOU A CLIMBER?

"The summit is what drives us,
but the climb itself is what matters"

—Conrad Anker

So, what kind of companies need a system like Pinnacle? Three types of businesses, which we will describe below.

In the first type of organization, the leadership team is frustrated and knows that they could be doing much better if they could only organize themselves and access a systematic approach to learning and implementing helpful tools and approaches. You may say that the leaders have a fear of missing out, and we call these "FOMO-frustrated" companies.

In the second type of business, the leadership team is highly ambitious. They want to become a category of one in their market segment. They want to build a business that is head and shoulders above its competitors, one that has a differentiated strategy underpinned by a stack of strategies that is hard for others to copy. We call these businesses "Domination-driven."

The third type of company has a leadership team that is 100 percent convinced there is a next level for them, and they need guidance to get there. These leaders and their businesses may be called "Improvement-inclined."

Besides belonging to one of the above categories, the Pinnacle journey is ideal for a business that is *privately held,* has *a coachable primary leader,* and a leadership team that is *open to new ideas,* willing to be *transparent* with each other, and *committed to growing* their business.

On the face of it, most businesses will fit the bill, so let's dissect this definition to be more specific.

Privately Held

A privately held business is one where the leadership has a vested interest in seeing the business succeed. Implementing a Pinnacle-type system requires the leadership members to step out of their comfort zone and grow as individuals.

Without owners whose livelihood depends on these decisions and who are personally connected to the business, the temptation is high for leadership to shy away from uncomfortable actions and decisions. For this reason, the system will take more effort to implement in nonprofit organizations and it would likely fail with a company under social or governmental control.

A seasoned CEO who had built multiple successful businesses in the food industry invited us to help a nonprofit where he was an activist board member. Other than being non-private, this organization was an ideal candidate for a system like Pinnacle. They had an inspiring mission, 25 employees, an experienced leadership team, plus a long history of operations that were well-funded by a loyal slate of donors.

Unfortunately, the Pinnacle system did not work for them. Only two members of their five-strong leadership team embraced the concept of growth and the idea of taking on more responsibility. The rest of the team, including the CEO, preferred the status quo of sandbagged plans, private fiefdoms, and a work–life balance tilted toward personal life focus.

Another type of organization where a Pinnacle-type system seems to not work as well is a venture-funded or private equity–backed company. We have seen three obstacles crop up in these types of organizations.

Venture-backed companies effectively hand over a bag of cash to a small group of bright, ambitious people who aim to build a fast-growth business that can quickly capture a new market niche. The founders tend to be young people with limited financial means, so almost all the money comes from investors. That creates a huge upside for the founders, who receive a salary and equity in the company, without much financial downside. (In the worst-case scenario, they lose their options and go look for another job.)

In this type of company, the founders are as much employees as they are entrepreneurs, and they split their focus between making the company more valuable and keeping their jobs. The latter requires them to keep the money flowing from the venture capitalists as the business (often unprofitably) scales, and to manage their relationship with the backers and fellow founders. Such a political dynamic can overwrite decisions that would normally be taken by owner-operators.

Private equity–funded companies tend to be more mature businesses that are already profitable. In these, management blueprints fail to get embraced for a different reason. Private equity fund managers are typically business school graduates, often with consulting backgrounds, and they fancy themselves more than just money men.

They believe that they possess all the business-building and strategy skills that their portfolio companies need to get to the next level. They are keen to provide it through their work on the board or as an assigned mentor to the leadership team.

In reality, however, these fund managers must focus their attention on finding other good companies to invest in before their fund's three- to five-year investment term expires, and on raising money for their next fund. The task of helping investee companies is often pushed to the back burner or receives less mental energy from these investment professionals than it deserves.

Open to New Ideas

It is a cliché that you cannot teach an old dog new tricks. We have found this to be true; however, we have also found that it is not the biological age of the dog that counts. We have seen middle-aged dogs that already "knew everything," while some of the senior canines we worked with were still in the "green and growing" phase. We like to say the fastest way to become an old dog is to stop learning new tricks.

Accepting the guidance of an external leadership team coach requires a degree of humility from a business owner who has already demonstrated their competence by having grown and sustained a business.

However, no intelligent CEO should be expected to blindly follow the guidance of an outsider. We agree with Aristotle, who said, "It is the mark of an educated mind to be able to entertain a thought without accepting it."

Early in his journey as a leadership coach, Steve was unaware of how important it was to avoid working with closed-minded clients. He came to realize that these business owners derived much of their job satisfaction from being the smartest person in the room and having people listen and applaud when they spoke.

Transparent

The objective of implementing Pinnacle is to create a team that can run the business. It is a team sport requiring you to develop people who can challenge each other and make better decisions together. This is not possible without your leadership team clearly understanding what is happening in your business, including the numbers in your profit and loss account and balance sheets.

If you are not willing to share financial details of how the business is doing, including its profitability, then it will be challenging to build trust with your team and allow them to understand what decisions need to be made to keep it growing and why.

Nevertheless, being transparent does not mean that you have to disclose individual salaries of executives and have the team discuss their bonuses with each other.

Coachable

It is natural that your experience will have taught you certain patterns that don't work, that are only distractions, or irrelevant.

You may even feel that you have seen it all: You've been in business for several decades, paid your dues, and would be unlikely to learn new information.

Different people also possess varying degrees of curiosity. As a busy business leader, you may have little bandwidth to pick up new information and would prefer to leverage the knowledge you already possess.

Whatever the reason, this material is designed for coachable individuals. You will benefit only to the degree that you believe that you *can* improve your game with a coach who brings a different perspective and experiences from other companies on how to grow and improve.

As Bill Gates explained in his 2013 TED Talk that went viral: "Everyone needs a coach. It doesn't matter whether you're a basketball player, a tennis player, a gymnast, or a bridge player. We all need people who will give us feedback. That's how we improve."[1]

We, and many other Pinnacle Business Guides, have worked with hundreds of businesses over our careers and have seen how companies succeed and fail. We are focused on detecting patterns and applying lessons taught by our own and our clients' challenges.

If you decide to work with a Pinnacle Business Guide, you can count on being pushed and having your assumptions challenged. A great guide is committed to growing your business and will not shy away from showing you the mirror and sharing examples of best practices from their other clients who have been where you are and have tackled similar challenges to yours. If you don't consider yourself coachable, hiring a guide will be a mistake and will lead to mutual frustration.

Committed to Growth

If you ask one hundred business owners whether they want their businesses to grow, ninety-eight will answer yes. However, the number of proprietors actually willing to pay the price of growth is much smaller.

Paraphrasing Michael Gerber, author of *The E-Myth*[2], most business owners are technicians and own a job rather than a company. Even when you have employees, you may treat the business as a way to make a comfortable living for yourself and your family rather than as a vehicle for growth. Growth requires stepping out of your comfort zone.

Why would you want to do the hard work of growth without a clear purpose waiting at the end of the rainbow, whether that is building a legacy, becoming wealthy, creating the conditions to self-actualize, or enjoying the fame and status of being a successful entrepreneur?

There is nothing wrong with being a lifestyle entrepreneur and trying to just keep the good times rolling without the pains of growth. But it makes no sense to implement a business operating system if you aren't aligned with these kinds of goals. You will just frustrate yourself and your people by pretending to support an expansion that you don't really want to be part of.

However, if your goal is to graduate from running your business to becoming a visionary entrepreneur as soon as possible, then Pinnacle is the ticket for you. Find someone who can be your Second in Command (2IC), someone you are willing to empower to run the business, and elevate yourself to the visionary position or even to the owner's box above it.

So, are you a climber?

If you are, then let's start climbing your first mountain: People!

MOUNTAIN ONE: PEOPLE

"*You don't build a business.*
You build people and then people build the business."

—**Zig Ziglar**

The first and foremost Pinnacle Principle is **People**. Every organization consists of people who are organized to create value for others. Great organizations expertly attract highly productive individuals who align with their culture. These people understand what contribution is expected of them and how they can consistently deliver on these expectations.

This chapter discusses the following topics:

1. How to define the type of people you need

2. How to attract these people and set expectations for them

3. How to help your people improve and grow over time so they become and remain A-Players who can be promoted to increasing responsibilities over time

The purpose of a business is to create and serve customers with needed products and services. Businesses do this through mobilizing resources such as people, capital, and tangible, intangible, and working capital assets.

The most important of these resources is your people because they directly leverage all the other assets mentioned above.

But in order for them to do that, as Jim Collins, author of *Good to Great*[3], states: "You need to get the right people on the bus and have them in the right seats and get the wrong people off the bus."

Collins further defines "right people" by saying, "The right people don't need to be tightly managed or fired up; they will be self-motivated by the inner drive to produce the best results and to be part of creating something great."[4] In other words, they are a great fit for your organizational **Culture**.

The right seats can be implied to mean the business **Functions** in which these people can productively execute their company's goals.

So, how do we define and measure *culture fit* and *productivity*, and what does **Coaching** people look like? This is what we will discuss as we explore the first mountain, the People Principle.

PRACTICE 1: CULTURE

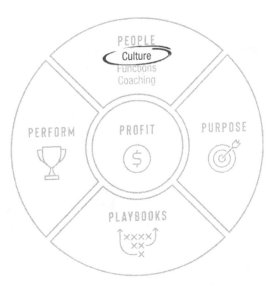

*"If you are lucky enough to be someone's employer,
then you have a moral obligation to make sure people do look
forward to coming to work in the morning."*

—John Mackey

Creating a strong culture for a business is critically important. Your culture is a set of beliefs, norms, and conducts that determine the behaviors and attitudes of your leadership members and your people with each other, with your customers, and with your vendors.

These inherent cultural and behavioral attributes are often called "core values," as coined by Jim Collins in *Beyond Entrepreneurship*.[5] We believe core values are not what large corporations like to adopt, such as "professionalism," "integrity," "teamwork," and so forth. We call these "corporate values," which are often too abstract, impersonal, or generic, which makes it hard to hold people accountable to them.

Typical corporate values feel more like vague aspirational statements than a description of how people actually behave in an organization. They certainly don't inform individuals of what they should be doing to exhibit such values.

Though these values may give people a sense of what the organization stands for, they are hardly actionable. What does it really take to manifest "professionalism," "integrity," or "teamwork," for example?

To get around this problem, companies often describe each core value, but do so in such a way that living up to them becomes impossible. If you search these terms online, you might find the following behaviors to describe them:

PROFESSIONALISM: neat appearance, proper demeanor (whatever these mean), reliability, competence, good communication, poise, being ethical, good phone etiquette, respecting others, being loyal, exceeding expectations, etc.

INTEGRITY: being gracious, respectful, honest, trustworthy, hardworking, responsible, helpful, patient, dependable, accountable, emotionally controlled, keeping promises, avoiding gossip, admitting mistakes, keeping confidences, showing up on time, following company policies, making hard decisions, etc.

TEAMWORK: trusts others, tolerant, self-aware, good listener, communicates clearly, responsible, honest, empathetic, collaborative, shows leadership, gives recognition, gives clear direction, defines roles, communicates openly, delegates effectively.

In other words, employees must be superhuman to live up to such perfectionist expectations.

Unfortunately, when you set unrealistic standards, you cannot live up to them yourself, and no one will take you seriously. Even if you were that godlike person, by setting unattainable standards, you let everyone else off the hook. Crazy rules don't count.

With all-encompassing corporate values like these, a company stands for everything; that is, it stands for nothing. It is much better to prioritize and select core values that describe a handful of virtues and behaviors that your employees can memorize and live up to.

The actual core values of a business tend to come from its founder or a handful of initial employees who established the business and brought it to its current level of success. (Remember the statistics: 50 percent of businesses don't survive beyond five years,[6] so being around is already a sign of success.)

Figure 1.1 Corporate vs Core Value Examples

CORPORATE VALUES vs CORE VALUES	
INTEGRITY	"Tells the Truth"
PROFESSIONALISM	"Respects Others"
TEAMWORK	"Has your back"

Core values are extremely important for scaling a business. The larger the organization, the more remote and diluted the impact of the founder's personality becomes. So, it is the core values of your company that transmit your—the founder's—values across the growing organization.

Identifying your company's core values requires focusing on its strengths and admitting that trade-offs are being made: core values have flip sides, and a business cannot be attractive to all kinds of employees and be all things to all customers.

The team at managed IT service provider Reliable Technologies Services (RTS) discovered during their culture articulation process that their core values empowered and limited them at the same time.

Their first core value, "Takes Ownership," implies that they are good at serving clients that treat them as a strategic partner. This means that clients with their own IT department, and those that only selectively farm out services that continue to be managed in-house, would be wrong fits for RTS.

Their second core value, "Expect Excellence," means that RTS provides a high-touch premium service offering rather than a cookie-cutter cloud service. The downside of being high-touch is that it is difficult to scale, and they should steer clear of low-budget clients who can't afford them.

Their third core value, "Communicates Well," underscores RTS's concierge approach. It means that they cannot hire geeks who only worry about the code. They must attract people who care about the customer and who are predisposed to being communicative. This core value suggests that people will be prioritized ahead of the product and that the culture prizes service ahead of innovation.

RTS's fourth core value, "Help First," transmits the fact that the company goes out of its way to help clients succeed as businesses, by proactively recommending productivity- and security-enhancing technology solutions. By "helping first" RTS employees subordinate their personal agendas to helping each other and clients. This business orientation attracts practically minded employees and might put off cutting-edge technologists.

Overall, RTS's core values describe a culture that focuses on customer service, fiduciary thinking, and strategic partnerships, rather than on building a product-oriented, scalable, technology-driven organization.

Here are other examples of how private companies express their unique DNAs through behavior-describing core values that make them successful:

- **Business development consulting firm** (all about delivering compelling, credible content):
  - Engages with content
  - Obsesses about the details
  - Learns continuously and strives for excellence

- o Shares and carries the load

- o Does whatever it takes

- **B2B software developer** (focused on authentic, flawless customer service)

  - o Problem solver

  - o Team oriented

  - o Acts with a sense of ownership

  - o Passionate about the customer experience

  - o Open and honest

- **Energy savings contractor** (obsessed with fast, clean, trouble-free installations)

  - o Takes Pride in Their Work

  - o Selflessly Supports the Team

  - o Treats Customers with Respect

An organization's core values orient employees to how they can be successful in the business. They also foster decision making and differentiate the company from its competitors. Adherence to core values across the organization creates a robust culture and a consistent customer experience.

Well-defined core values help attract and promote employees that fit your culture at the same time as identifying culture misfits, who then can be asked to align their behavior or leave the organization.

Unearthing Your Company's Core Values

Jim Collins came up with an exercise for businesses to discover their core values called The Mars Group.[7] Key employees were asked to identify the five to seven people who best embodied the values of their organization and who would therefore be the company's prime ambassadors on a mission to Mars.

After listing ambassadors, the group describes the attributes and attitudes of these people that make them so appropriate for the role. Participants often come up with thirty to forty behaviors, which can then be whittled down to a handful, preferably four to six core values.

If your organization has already defined its core values, ask the team whether they remember them and love them. If the answer is no to either question, you might be well served starting over again with the Mars Group exercise and defining behavior-based values instead.

If the leadership knows and loves your corporate values, ask them to describe the behaviors that manifest those values. What does it look like when somebody demonstrates "engaging with content," "being a problem solver," or "performing consistently" in your organization? In all likelihood, you will receive a handful of responses from which you can negotiate down to the best one or two descriptions of each core value.

Having four to six core values is the sweet spot. This number gives you enough depth while at the same time are few enough so that your people can memorize and internalize them.

Lencioni's Core Value Traps

In the *Harvard Business Review* article "Make Your Values Mean Something,"[8] Patrick Lencioni discusses three "value traps" that companies tend to fall into when articulating their core values:

1. **Permission-to-play (or "table stakes") core values.** They pick values that represent the minimum standard for any company of their type and that do not differentiate them. "Detail oriented" would be a permission-to-play virtue for a CPA firm but may be core for a construction business that has a hard time finding supervisors who can follow a room-finish drawing.

2. **Accidental core values**. These are values that may have been important in the past but are no longer relevant or even helpful. Being "entrepreneurial" is critical for a startup but can get in the way while scaling a company. At that stage, people who can follow Playbooks are more important than survivalists and idea people who get bored with business as usual.

3. **Aspirational core values**. These are the most dangerous types of values. The ones that you would desperately like to exhibit, but don't.

Avoid these value traps by scrutinizing your potential core values for signs of any falling in one of the above categories. Your core values are those four to six success behaviors that your best people exhibit and that are already inherent, relevant, and non-generic for your business. (See Figure 1.2.) Your Pinnacle Business Guide is an expert at helping you pick relevant, inspiring, and unique core values while avoiding all the traps.

Figure 1.2 Core Value Filter

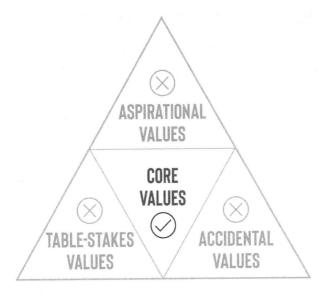

In his earlier book *Buyable*,[9] Steve tells the story of the nonprofit that reluctantly picked the value "Tells the truth" upon the insistence of its freshly minted CEO. This value turned out to be an aspirational one, and the leadership team broke out in open revolt against being held accountable to it.

More recently, a former client insisted on having "Communicates authentically and listens to understand" as a core value, even though multiple leadership team members admitted that they didn't actually practice that behavior. We could not talk them out of picking it as a core value for their company, and the C-suite continued to struggle with a credibility deficit with employees.

Pick the values that really describe you, and let the people who can wholeheartedly embrace your culture choose to work for your organization. You will not like or tolerate other types anyway.

Be transparent about who you are and what your business is about in your job advertisements and in interviews. Publicly recognize individual employees with specifics for living your organization's core values and ask your people to do the same for each other in all-hands meetings.

Fodder for Constructive Conversations

Having a handful of clearly defined core values helps your employees self-select and orient their behaviors.

Well-defined core values also allow you to address any behavioral issues when they arise. If you see one of your people not living your core values, e.g., they are not "Acting with a sense of ownership," point it out to them. Discuss what you have witnessed or heard about, and coach them to understand how they should have handled the situation.

It helps to have a couple of examples handy to affirm a pattern of core value failure, rather than an exception. Have your employee own the issue and ask them to commit to fixing their behavior. Keep an eye on this person and follow up in a month or so to give them feedback.

Most people accept this kind of specific feedback and are grateful for it after they have some time for reflection. But some will not change, and you will be forced to make a decision. Be ready with a succession plan when the moment of truth arrives.

Enforcing your organization's core values is the most potent tool for perpetuating the culture you have infused into your organization. Be vigilant with reinforcing it. Just as your grandkids are the mirror of how well you did as a parent, your company culture's effectiveness is a reflection of how well your core values are in play.

Key Ideas from Practice 1: Culture

- Individual behaviors—not abstract corporate values—drive companies. Pick core values that describe how your best employees act for the benefit of the organization.

- Your organization's core values are the tools you use to articulate and scale the company's culture.

- Avoid Lencioni's value traps by applying the Core Value Filter.

- Leaders must exhibit and model your core values for them to carry weight with your employees.

Shortly, we will discuss how to evaluate people's adherence to your core values, but let's first talk about how to structure your organization.

PRACTICE 2: FUNCTIONS

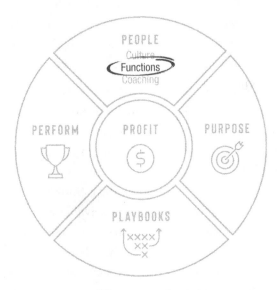

"Organize around business functions, not people.
Build systems within each business function.
Let systems run the business and people run the systems."

—Michael Gerber

All businesses are different. Some focus on manufacturing, some on agricultural production, others on software development or retail. Fundamentally, however, all businesses have three imperatives, namely to Get Work, to Do Work, and to Get Paid.[10] No business can stand stable if any of these three legs of the stool are missing.

Getting Work is all about creating new customers and generating more business from existing customers by selling them products or services. Without customers and revenues, there is no life in the corporate body. Examples of functions that fulfill the Get Work function are marketing, thought leadership, sales, estimating, business development, and strategic partnering.

Doing Work is creating the value that your customers are willing to pay for. It can include delivering services or creating and distributing physical or digital products that you have produced or licensed. It also includes servicing your existing customers and solving any problems that may arise. If a business doesn't Do Work, customers will disappear. Doing Work is manifested by such functions as delivery, customer service, product development, software development, engineering, consulting, operations, etc.

The third leg of the stool is Getting Paid. No matter how many happy customers you create and serve, you must also get paid for your products or services in a timely fashion, or you run out of cash and will be out of business soon. The functions that ensure you Get Paid involve all the administrative back-office work, including bookkeeping, accounting, financial control, invoicing, accounts receivable and payable, payroll, recruiting, office management, technology and telecom infrastructure, vehicles, legal, insurance, and purchasing. No matter how much new business you generate, no matter how excellent the quality of the work you deliver to customers, if you don't get paid, you will eventually go bankrupt.

Get Work, Do Work, and Get Paid are all equally important. They are the essence of your business. (See Figure 2.1.)

Figure 2.1: Function Finder Chart

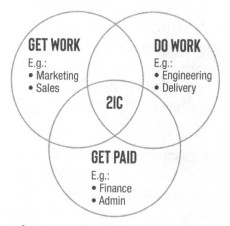

Source: Concept adapted from Pinnacle Business Guide, Keith Trost.

Years ago, we advised a fast-growing and profitable contracting company that developed a cash flow issue that almost put it out of business. They had two business units: one provided water and fire damage mitigation and restoration services; the other, general contracting to rebuild flooded bathrooms and burnt-out kitchens.

The restoration business was cash-healthy because insurance companies made reimbursements in a timely manner. However, the rebuild division built up high receivables balances because customers paid slowly for services not covered by insurance.

After taking out a credit line and running into credit card debt, the owner of the business finally had to face up to having a structural issue. The rebuild division was not getting paid fast enough to finance its own growth.

To reverse this situation, the company would have had to become more profitable by raising its prices, but insurance companies channeled business to low-price providers, so this was not an option in this insurance-driven business model.

The solution was to scale back the rebuild business and keep it at a slow growth rate while asking for up-front deposits and selectively taking on new clients. Having a lower volume of business also allowed the company to let go of its less-productive project managers and keep the ones who kept projects on time and on budget.

So, what if your company gets a lot of business and gets paid, but doesn't do the work? Clearly, this mode of operation would create unhappy customers, negative Yelp reviews, and an escalating cost of generating new customers, putting you out of business.

Similarly, being great at Doing Work and Getting Paid but weak in Getting Work can sustain your business for a while but causes big problems in the long term.

For example, a marketing agency we worked with years ago suffered from a Get Work problem. This did not bother them for a long time, because their clients were growing by leaps and bounds. The three clients they had picked up in the early stage of the practice have grown into nine-figure companies, giving the agency more organic growth than it could handle without new logos coming in. The marketing firm grew from two partners to a staff of 30 professionals over a period of 15 years.

At some point, however, one of the customers, a national chain of photography studios, was disrupted by smartphone photography and went into Chapter 11.

The agency was then down to two major customers, one of which was acquired a year later by a national competitor. The buyer had its own agency relationship and dumped our client. Suddenly, this business was unviable, with over 60 percent of revenues coming from a single client.

The owner tried to figure out how to generate new business, but the sales engine was completely missing from the company. It simply could not compete for new clients with similar-sized firms. The owner decided to outsource the business and close down his agency.

Make sure you have functions that operationalize all three legs of the stool: Get Work, Do Work, and Get Paid.

The Functions You Need

We define a **Function** as an area of responsibility that needs to be owned and developed by an executive-level employee in your business. Each business needs to define at least one function for each of the Get Work, Do Work, Get Paid operations, most typically sales, delivery, and administration, that report to the CEO or a second in command (2IC) if leadership is split between an entrepreneurial leader and a person who runs day-to-day activities.

Gino Wickman, the author of *Traction*,[11] calls the executives in this split leadership arrangement the Visionary and the Integrator, respectively. Small companies rarely split the leadership position, but entrepreneurial founders often want to elevate themselves out of the day-to-day management of the business in order to focus on competitive issues, strategic relationships, onboarding investors, and making acquisitions.

When a CEO has removed themselves from the day-to-day operations, we call this person the Visionary and the person who runs the business the 2IC.

Smaller firms often only have three functions reporting to an owner/ CEO, whereas larger businesses might have five to seven major functions reporting to a 2IC, who in turn reports to, or works shoulder-to-shoulder with, an entrepreneurial CEO.

The Visionary and the 2IC are ideally the ying and yang of the business. The Visionary tends to be outside-oriented, often a charismatic individual, who focuses on spreading the company's message and finding new ways to grow the business, conquering new markets, building strategic partnerships, and formulating strategy.

The 2IC concentrates on minding the shop and making sure the executive group works as a team and executes the plan, the employees are happy, and that the business makes its revenue and profit numbers.

Function Ownership Chart

The Function Ownership Chart is a forward-looking document that sketches out the requirements for your next level of growth. (See Figure 2.2.) This may involve multiple functions being owned by a single executive; for example, start-up entrepreneurs often begin wearing most of the hats. However, no function can be owned by multiple executives because that eliminates clear accountability for that function.

The Pinnacle System works when you have at least three leadership-level executives who can solve problems and develop plans together. The goal is to develop increased autonomy so that the CEO or 2IC can delegate tasks and focus on the highest value-add activities that cannot yet be delegated.

Dan Sullivan, founder of Strategic Coach, calls these your "Unique Ability."[12] According to Sullivan, the key to great delegation is to shed all functions that you can hire out or teach others to do for you. This then allows you to focus your time and energy on the areas where you create the most value and where replacing you would be the most expensive, most risky, or most complex.

For a Visionary, with a 2IC running the day-to-day, unique abilities could include thought leadership, strategic relationship, mergers and acquisitions, and new markets.

Figure 2.2: Function Ownership Chart

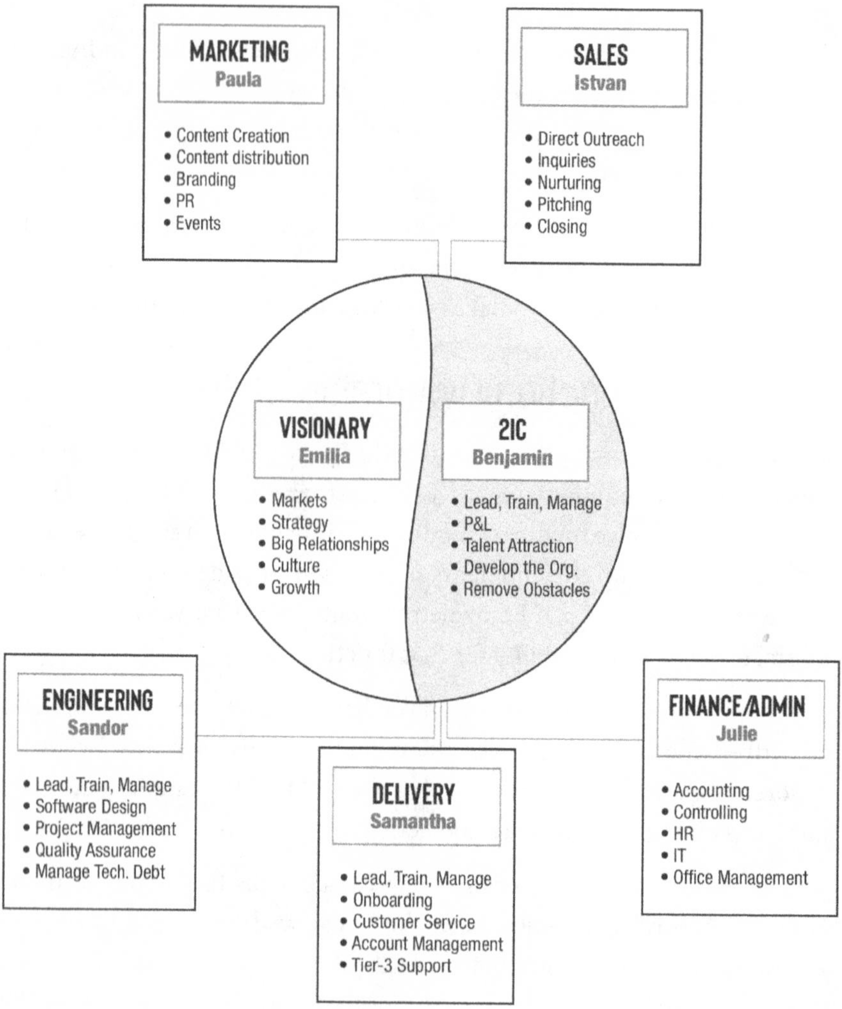

MARKETING
Paula

- Content Creation
- Content distribution
- Branding
- PR
- Events

SALES
Istvan

- Direct Outreach
- Inquiries
- Nurturing
- Pitching
- Closing

VISIONARY
Emilia

- Markets
- Strategy
- Big Relationships
- Culture
- Growth

2IC
Benjamin

- Lead, Train, Manage
- P&L
- Talent Attraction
- Develop the Org.
- Remove Obstacles

ENGINEERING
Sandor

- Lead, Train, Manage
- Software Design
- Project Management
- Quality Assurance
- Manage Tech. Debt

DELIVERY
Samantha

- Lead, Train, Manage
- Onboarding
- Customer Service
- Account Management
- Tier-3 Support

FINANCE/ADMIN
Julie

- Accounting
- Controlling
- HR
- IT
- Office Management

We call this diagram the Function Ownership Chart because it depicts the major functions that the business needs to become independent from its owner and grow to the next level. The executive who owns a function becomes accountable for delivering the three to five most important outcomes for that function, listed with bullet points below the name of each function in Figure 2.2.

Outcomes differ from business to business, but for the Sales function of a housebuilder, the outcomes may be: lead generation, estimating, negotiating, and handoff, whereas the Sales function of a consulting business may include: content creation, lead generation, new business, and account management outcomes, etc.

The Operations function of a housebuilder may include outcomes such as: scheduling, project management, and punch list completion, whereas the consulting business may define the outcomes of its Operations function as: scoping, project management, subcontractors, and delivery.

The Administration function's typical outcomes at a smaller firm are finance, HR, IT, and office management.

Determine who should run each function based on their ability and commitment to execute on the outcomes and deliver the results you need.

Everyone Is Doing Everything

Some time ago, we advised a general contracting company. Its founder and CEO wanted to turn it into a scalable business, but one of the bottlenecks to scaling was the company's organizational structure.

Rather than being organized by autonomous functions, such as Sales, Operations, and Administration, the company was structured as a professional services partnership. The three senior people in the organization, including the CEO, had their own client portfolios, and each of them also managed large projects themselves. As a result, there was no management capacity left at the leadership level, and the company was stuck at around $30 million in annual sales.

Each senior partner was responsible for getting and executing work, hiring and managing people and projects, and maintaining profitability. That created a feast or famine cycle because the partners were absorbed by project management interspersed with chasing work when the well ran dry.

Worse, most decisions had to be made by the CEO, who was the only person who could arbitrate between the partners, who then felt out of control in servicing their clients.

The goal of creating functions is to foster autonomy and growth by setting expectations and creating accountability. We like to think of function owners as "mini-CEOs" who are empowered to make the most of their function by building and coaching their teams, getting results, and improving processes, which we call Playbooks. (More on that in Mountain Three: Playbooks.)

Win-the-Week Scoreboard

So, how do you know that your function owners are delivering the results you need? Well, that is where weekly metrics come in. (Metrics are discussed in depth in Practice 11: Metrics, later in the book.) How do you know if you had a great week in sales? Have you made four customer demos, which you expect to create two proposals? Have you issued two proposals that will lead to a sale? Did you write two blog posts that you expect to generate five new leads?

The idea of weekly metrics is to keep your team on track with achieving results in real time. Accountants tend to be skeptical of this approach because they are used to measuring performance retrospectively, when all the information is in for the month or the quarter. The trouble is that financial statements are rarely available before the 15th of the month following the quarter, by which time you may be six weeks behind in some areas, making it too late to course-correct.

Start by developing two metrics for each function owner that, if hit, would prove they had a great week. Taken together, these metrics represent your Win-the-Week Scoreboard. (See Figure 2.3.)

Figure 2.3 Win-the-Week Scoreboard

FUNCTION	OWNER	OUTCOMES	METRICS	TARGET/WEEK	RESULTS	METER	WON?
VISIONARY	Emilia	# of followers Market share Market cap	# of big relationships touched # of talks, interviews, blogs	3 2	4 1		Y N
2IC	Benjamin	Profit Cash flow	# of coaching conversations # of talent prospect conversations	5 2	5 3		Y Y
MARKETING	Paula	Lead flow Social media engagement Brand awareness	# of qualified leads # of content pieces distributed	4 3	2 3		N Y
SALES	Istvan	Sales revenue New logos acquired	# of proposals issued $ of new MRR contracted	3 $5,000	2 $5,500		N Y
ENGINEERING	Sandor	Regular new releases Happy users	# of open tickets Staff utilization %	<=5 80%	2.5% 75%		Y N
DELIVERY	Samantha	Gross profit Growing existing customers	# of hours billed # of business reviews	600 2	625 0		Y N
FINANCE/ADMIN	Julie	Quickbooks is accurate & up to date Helpful and updated Scoreboards	$ of invoices issued Receivable days	$160,000 30	$180,000 42		Y Y
WON THE WEEK?							9/5

Avoiding Burnout

An important byproduct of drawing up a Function Ownership Chart and a Win-the-Week Scoreboard is that you will clearly see whether an executive is overwhelmed. If so, it is then time to add someone to their team or prioritize by taking less-important items off their plate.

If there is no budget available for hiring, you can outsource to freelancers (check out Upwork.com), delegate to technology (is there an app for that?), or create a "stop doing list." Remember the Pareto principle[13]: 20 percent of actions drive 80 percent of results. Inversely, 20 percent of your team's activities likely deliver negligible value and can be eliminated without anyone complaining.

Key Ideas from Practice 2: Functions

- The basic jobs of any business are to Get Work, Do Work, and to Get Paid.

- Determine the major Functions that accomplish these three basic jobs in your business and define the outcomes they need to deliver.

- Who is the right person to deliver on the outcomes and results of each of your Functions?

- Find one or two metrics for each Function that evidence that its most critical outcomes are being delivered.

Now that we have defined the core values to exhibit and the outcomes and results to deliver for each member of your leadership team and your organization, let's talk about whom and how to coach to develop the talent in your business.

PRACTICE 3: COACHING

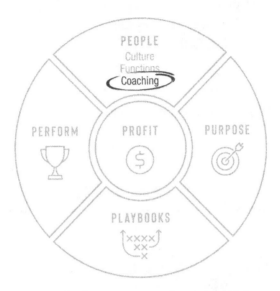

"Coaching is unlocking a person's potential to maximize their own performance. It's helping them to learn, rather than teaching them."

—Tim Gallwey

By picking behavior-based core values, we have determined your company's Culture and established its major and minor Functions and the people who own them. It is now time to assess your talent pool.

You need to evaluate and understand who your A-Players are so you can empower and promote them; who your A-Potentials are who need more coaching to grow into A-Players; and whether you have any B- and C-Players who might need your attention or decision.

The Talent Assessment chart comes from Verne Harnish's Scaling Up program. With this simple tool, you can quickly and simply evaluate your people along two dimensions: (1) How well they fit your culture; and (2) How consistently productive they are in their current role.

Culture fit is simply an assessment on a scale of 1 to 10 of whether the person lives your organization's core values. If they live and breathe all your values all the time, they are a 10. If they exhibit half your core values all the time and the other half never, or they demonstrate all your values half the time, they are a 5, and so forth.

Assessing productivity works the same way. People who are consistently highly productive deserve a 9 or a 10. Those who miss deadlines, require nudging, need regular help, or the like, should get a lower score.

Figure 3.1 Talent Assessment chart

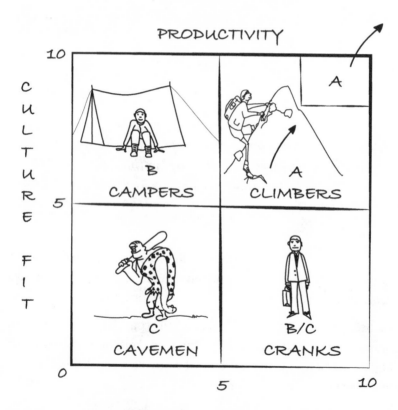

Source: Concept adapted from Verne Harnish's Scaling Up program.

Associates who score a 9 or a 10 on both their culture fit and productivity are your A-Players. They are your best people—the 20 percent who produce 80 percent of the results—so take good care of them.

We call your employees that score over 6 on both dimension, but less than 9 on one or two of them, your A-Potentials. They are not your best yet, but they are likely worth your time and attention to try to boost them to A-Player territory.

People who score 6–10 on culture and 1–5 on productivity are your "campers." They are likable and fun, but they tend to fall behind in their work. Campers are great people to share a beer and a story with around the campfire, but don't count on them to raise tents or cook dinner. They are your B-Players, and they can become a time suck. Beware.

You B/C-Players are those who score 1–5 on culture fit and 6–10 on productivity. They get the job done but can be toxic to your culture, as they don't get along with their colleagues or they spend time politicking. We call these people "cranks" because they are only happy in their own bubble and rarely embrace being part of a team.

Cranks can be dangerous because their negative tendencies might stay hidden and poison your organization in unseen ways. At the same time, their productivity is addictive and difficult to replace. It's better to make a tough decision sooner than grow dependent on them.

One of our clients, a construction company, faced the issue of dependence on a toxic team member. He was a smart and ambitious individual who quickly rose through the ranks to become the head of customer delivery. He recruited his subordinates, who did a good job, but many of them could not speak English and relied on him for all communications with clients and coworkers.

Over time, the team grew to such an extent that he became a bottleneck, and work started to slow down, disappointing customers. To improve communications, the leadership team proposed splitting his role and appointing a customer success manager. But he became defensive about the change, which he feared might infringe on his autonomy and reduce his control over his departmental "empire."

Eventually, he quit the organization and enticed several people who had reported to him to follow him to another company, at a great disruption to our client. He was a "crank," and he cost this company in the end.

Being an A-Player is role dependent. The proverbial sales superstar who fails when promoted to sales manager is a case in point. On the other hand, A-Players should be the prime candidates for promotion because they have learned to excel in a role and they are more likely than their less accomplished colleagues to repeat that pattern in the face of bigger responsibilities.

Your A-Players end up being free, because they pay for themselves, and there is even money left over.

People who score 5 or less on both culture fit and productivity are your C-Players, whom we call "cavemen," as they are both unliked and unproductive. Hopefully, you don't have any, but if you do, you have no time to waste. Such people are actively destroying your organization, as we speak, so don't lose time trying to fix them.

The Socratic Method

In our postindustrial economy, chances are that your most important assets are your people. This is the case even if you own valuable physical or intellectual properties, because even these depend on your people for harvesting and preservation.

Consequently, growing your business is all about growing the capacities of your people. The smarter and more skilled your associates become, the more you will be able to hand off to them and focus on strategy and growth.

Your top job after picking great people is to coach and mentor them. **Coaching** means helping them grow by asking thought-provoking questions rather than handing them ready-made solutions. This style of leadership is often called the Socratic method.

Asking questions so that your people can figure things out is harder than making the decisions yourself. Especially if you are an impatient entrepreneurial leader. In the short term, it will also lead to mistakes while your people learn to make good decisions on their own. Resist the temptation to abandon this approach.

You can mitigate the risk by applying Susan Scott's tree method of decision making.[14] Think of the different types of decisions made in your organization as representing the roots, the trunk, the branches, and the leaves of a tree.

"Leaf" decisions are the ones that your direct reports can make without your knowledge. For example, if you own a customer service company, your representatives have been trained on and should be able to decide which standard products to offer customers. They may make a mistake every once in a while, but it can be corrected easily without much risk to the business.

Figure 3.2 Susan Scott's Decision Tree

DECISION	DIRECT REPORT	LEADER	EXAMPLE
Leaf	Decides alone	–	Product recommendation
Branch	Decides alone	Informed	Discretionary spending to address client complaint
Trunk	Joint decision	Joint decision	Raise for team member of direct report
Root	–	Decides alone	Raise for direct report

A "branch" decision is a second-level decision, still low risk, but you want to know about decision making at this level so you can course-correct if necessary. Your direct reports make branch-level decisions but inform you of them.

A "trunk" decision is made together with your direct reports. You take their input and coach them toward figuring out the right decision under your control.

Finally, there are "root" decisions that you make on your own, without the involvement of employees, although you might seek their input beforehand.

Creating Leaders

The first Pinnacle Principle is People, and your number one job as the owner of the business is to build a leadership team.

Leaders spend their time getting things done *through* others instead of executing the work themselves. Moving from doing to leading requires your employees to make a mental shift: They have to trade doing the work, which they are likely already good at, for finding, attracting, and empowering others to do it for them.

You empower people by defining the Functions of the organization and the expected outcomes for each function and then assigning owners to each Function. This creates an opening for each function owner to manifest that function and to support their function to the best of their abilities and the resources they can negotiate.

Leaders also make decisions. Deciding means cutting off or killing alternatives so that the decision maker can move forward without fragmenting their focus and resources.

For example, getting married is a decision to stop dating other people and to dedicate your energy and resources to building a life with the chosen person and possibly having a family. Can you imagine the complexity of managing multiple families with partners who are splitting their attention the same way?

So, making decisions is essential to managing resources. But it is hard work, as it involves accepting the loss of some choices and taking responsibility for the risk that your decision might not work out and your credibility might take a hit.

Of course, it is hard to make decisions when your mental energy is dissipated by "doing". To emerge as a leader, you must step out of the comfort of doing work you have already mastered, and step into the painful and risky work of leadership. You will have to coach your leadership team to do the same.

Moreover, a leader can only let go of work to others who have not yet mastered the task by simultaneously training and coaching them to become effective. Training and holding people accountable are part of the job of a leader.

"Bring Me Two Solutions"

You will find that your A-Players will embrace decision-making, while most others will continue to bring you problems. Condition your assistance on whether the employee brings two or more potential solutions for each problem. You will soon find that they can choose the right decision themselves, without you, when they have been coached on their Function and know the expected outcomes.

Having daily Standup meetings (more of that in Practice 12: Meetings) conditions employees to ask for help at a specific time of day, rather than in an ad hoc fashion. This practice forces less-patient employees to make more decisions on their own.

You can further foster decision making by allowing for first-time mistakes. As long as someone doesn't commit the same mistake twice, your direct reports should be allowed to fail at making branch-level decisions. You will be informed, of course, and thus can intervene as necessary.

Peer Problem Solving

You can also teach leadership team members to solve issues by modeling it in meetings. Ask people to bring their problems and opportunities to weekly tactical meetings. Here, your team can prioritize and solve these topics together by identifying root causes and deciding on the best solution by harvesting the team's problem-solving power.

While running the meeting, you can model how to prioritize, analyze, evaluate, and solve problems. (More on this in Mountain Four: Perform.)

The magic of peer problem solving is that it invokes the "mastermind principle," a term first coined by Napoleon Hill in the mega bestseller, since the 1930s, *Think and Grow Rich*.[15] Hill describes how successful business entrepreneurs and CEOs cultivate a brain trust of smart and curious problem solvers with diverse experiences around them, to generate ideas and solutions.

By implanting the habit of peer problem solving at different levels of your business, you are connecting your people like a giant computer network and tapping into the collective brain power of your organization. This human "supercomputer" will help you solve problems at lower levels in your business, freeing up the bandwidth of top and middle management for higher-level and strategic thinking.

Mentor Meetings

Another forum for coaching your direct reports is in structured quarterly Mentor Meetings. Initially, you may need to use these type of meetings more frequently than that, but over time your people will learn to solve problems and make decisions on their own and with their peers in daily and weekly meetings.

By scheduling one-on-one time at least quarterly, you create a structure for feedback and learning, decoupled from annual compensation reviews.

Figure 3.1 Mentor Meetings

The goals of the Mentor Meeting are twofold. On the one hand, this quarterly exchange is an opportunity for direct reports to get your help as their mentor in becoming more successful in their job and career.

On the other hand, it gives you the opportunity to provide employees with feedback on how well they live your organization's core values and how well they are delivering on the outcomes in their function. This is also a good time to clarify mutual expectations of both the mentor and the mentee and re-energize the relationship.

Key Ideas from Practice 3: Coaching

- Evaluate your people on culture fit and productivity to determine who are your A-Players, A-Potentials, and B- and C-players.

- Focus on developing A-Potentials and promoting A-Players so that they deliver more for your business and don't get bored. Consider replacing B- and B/C- Players. (Let any Cs go immediately.)

- Build a coaching culture at your organization by practicing the Socratic method, the tree method of decision making, pushing people to make decisions, peer problem solving, and having quarterly Mentor Meetings with each employee.

Messages from Mountain One: People

Articulating your **Culture**, who you and your business are, and your unique way of being successful, allows for scalability. Defining your company's core values gives you a way to ingrain and perpetuate your company's culture.

Clarify the **Functions** that your business needs to accomplish to get to the next level on the way to the Pinnacle. Define expectations and empower your people as mini-CEOs to grow their respective functions.

Your most valuable resource is your people. The growth of your company cannot exceed the quality of your executives, including yourself, so you need **Coaching** for everyone to reach increasingly higher levels of impact.

For example, in less than two years, e-commerce consulting company Groove Commerce groomed two outstanding leaders by promoting individuals who embodied its culture, setting expectations on how they should lead, and giving them ownership of decisions.

These leaders felt empowered to think about their respective functions more strategically, documenting processes and coaching others to delegate many of their day-to-day activities. This in turn opened up their calendars to engage on the leadership team and start new initiatives for the company.

Now that you have defined the right culture for your company and expectations for your employees, empowered the right people to lead, and established a system of growing your people through one-on-one and peer coaching, it's time to give your business a Purpose.

MOUNTAIN TWO: PURPOSE

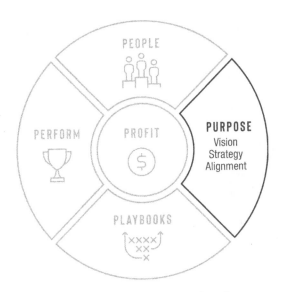

"When you're surrounded by people who share a passionate commitment around a common purpose, anything is possible."

—Howard Schultz

Every business has to have a purpose and provide a societal good for which others are willing to pay.

Why not, then, pick an inspiring purpose that your people can be excited about? If you can do that, you will turn your employees into missionaries who are emotionally invested in making your business successful.

They will not only bring their time and skills to your company but also happily mobilize their mental and emotional energies well beyond the value of their paychecks. Because they want to.

Jeff Bezos, Founder of Amazon, spoke about wanting to work with such "missionaries" rather than "mercenaries." Missionaries need a galvanizing purpose they can stand behind. Your job is to articulate one.

The Pinnacle Principle of Purpose has three distinct practices: Vision, Strategy, and Alignment. Let's dive in to explore what these are, and how to engineer them into your business.

PRACTICE 4: VISION

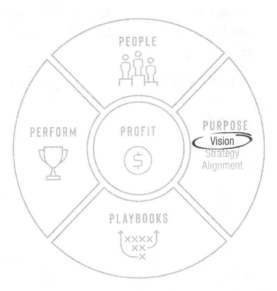

"Putting in long hours for a corporation is hard.
Putting in long hours for a cause is easy."

—Elon Musk

Every business needs three types of **Vision** for maximum effectiveness. The first vision is an enduring, long-term objective, a powerful aspiration. This is the "Why," or the reason for the organization to exist, and it could remain unchanged for one hundred years or more, even as the market and the company's core business change.

The second type of vision is what Jim Collins and Jerry Porras called the "Big Hairy Audacious Goal (BHAG)."[16] This is the long-term, tangible "What" of your business on a seven- to twenty-year time horizon. We call this your Pinnacle.

The third type of vision is a vivid depiction of what your business would look like three to five years into the future, on its way toward your Pinnacle. One way to do that is to teleport your people into the medium-term future in their minds and ask them to look back on their journey and describe the milestones they had to hit along the way.

We call this vision your Medium-term Milestones, to emphasize that these are broad-brush accomplishments that will have been achieved by your selected three- to five-year target date.

After your vision has been clearly defined, it's time to define your "How," which is the Strategy that will enable you to reach your Medium-term Milestones and ultimately your Pinnacle.

Your job as the leader is to create Alignment around your organization's Vision and Strategy.

It is imperative that you paint a compelling reason and future for your organization that is worth striving for. Together with your leadership team, figure out how you will get there and sell everyone on that plan, so that all the human energy of your business is channeled toward achieving your organization's Vision.

Your Company's Why

Some years ago, the president of a linen laundry company joined a CEO peer group that Steve ran. He lamented about his struggles to recruit talented executives to run his business, which he admitted was one that operated in an unappealing industry, handling dirty linens and working in uncomfortably humid and hot environments. "Who would be attracted to join such a business?" he asked rhetorically.

But his fellow CEOs got curious and, during the ensuing discussion, unearthed that his business indeed had an inspiring Why: The linen company's hotel customers and hospital patients appreciated the comfort of clean linens. Further, the company's policy of using low-impact detergents helped preserve the environment.

Shortly after this discovery, the company's vision was revised to reflect its positive Why and the impact the company was making in the world. Within the next six months, the organization attracted two highly qualified

C-level executives, rejuvenating the business. Finding a compelling Why can bring success quickly as everyone aligns with that vision and strives to bring it about.

Motivational speaker and author Simon Sinek states in his widely watched YouTube video "Start with Why"[17] that what matters to both your customers and your employees is *why* you do what you do more than *what* you actually do. He makes the case that Apple's popularity stemmed from people's desire to be the customer of a business that they could relate to. People choose Apple for emotional reasons more than for logical ones.

Ideas can be extremely powerful; people can be willing to die for them, let alone merely join your company. Lincoln and Churchill changed world history by passionately pursuing ideas they fervently believed in, however unaccomplishable those ideas appeared to be to most people, at the time.

The republic of the United States has survived 245 years on the basis of the Lockean ideas of the unalienable right to "Life, Liberty, and the Pursuit of Happiness." Similarly, your company's Why is a powerful motivating force for your people.

Crafting an inspiring Why is one of the biggest opportunities for your business. It will help you galvanize your employees, attract A-Players, and release the pent-up mental and emotional energy of the people in your organization.

A few iconic corporate Whys include the following:

- "To accelerate the world's transition to sustainable energy."[18] —Tesla
- "To save our home planet."[19] —Patagonia
- "To create more joyful lives through better health."[20] —Walgreens Boots Alliance
- "To make humanity multi-planetary to survive a potential catastrophe on Earth."[21] —SpaceX
- "To create a future of zero crashes, zero emissions, and zero congestion."[22] —GM

- "To create a more positive narrative around Africa."[23] —EbonylifeTV

Here are a few examples from small companies we have worked with:

- "To build the future of commerce." —Groove Commerce
- "To empower human potential with the tools of tomorrow." —LookThink
- "To advance life at home." —Atlas Home Energy Solutions
- "To return free time to accountants." —Adriana Accounting
- "To build positive relationships" —BankVista
- "To Inform People About Their Health" —Veravas (antibody detection)

Naturally, not everyone will resonate with your Why, and some people may not be excited by your company's purpose and decide to leave. However, this can be a good thing because it gives you the opportunity to replace them with "missionaries," who will passionately support what your business is all about.

Finding Your Company's Why

Finding your Why is about tapping into the emotion of why we ultimately do what we do.

Keep in mind that the company's Why is not about your product or service. It is much bigger and more enduring than that—it's something that your business would be able to pursue well beyond your long-term goals.

A good way to figure out the Why of your company is to apply a root cause analysis and drill down five levels asking why. By peeling the onion and staying curious, you can get to the fundamental reason why your organization exists.

When we worked on discovering the Why for Atlas Home Energy Solutions (AHES), the conversation went something like this:

Why does AHES exist?

To help homeowners improve the energy efficiency of their homes.

Why is improving energy efficiency important?

To make our customers' homes more comfortable, reduce their energy bills, and ensure they breathe clean air.

Why are these things important for your customers?

So that they enjoy their home more, save money, stay healthy, and help preserve our environment.

Why is this important to the people at AHES?

Because we want to improve the lives of our customers.

How would you state that as a unified idea that would stay true for one hundred years even if your services changed over time?

*Whatever changes, we would still want **"To Advance Life at Home."***

In this example, four whys were enough to get to the core, and the fifth question was designed to synthesize and articulate the idea into a more general form.

It can help to use a Pinnacle Business Guide to find your Why because you may be too close to your company to see what is really happening under the surface.

Figure 4.1 Pinnacle Pyramid Part 1: Vision

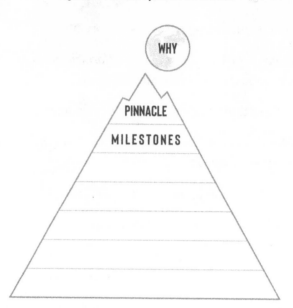

What Is Your Pinnacle?

In May 1961, President John F. Kennedy addressed both houses of Congress and proposed a plan to put a man on the moon before the end of the decade and return him safely to Earth.

This was a visionary statement that spurred a drifting NASA and the whole country behind an audacious mission to regain the initiative in the Cold War and reinforce the global supremacy of the United States.

The concept of the Big Hairy Audacious Goal, or BHAG, is to articulate an exciting and worthwhile goal that can get people's juices flowing in an organization. We call this the **Pinnacle** that your business is climbing toward.

The time frame of the Pinnacle has to be long enough—typically 7 to 20 years—to allow for visionary thinking while still being tangible enough for most people to realistically strive for during their potential tenure at your company.

The Pinnacle represents the "What" that your organization is striving for. It is a milestone along the journey toward your Why.

Business owners often struggle with defining a Pinnacle that falls beyond their personal time horizon at the company. If the founder wants to exit in three years, they will hardly relate to a 10-year Pinnacle. However, a successful exit depends on an engaged workforce that believes in the company even after the founder is gone. So, articulating a Pinnacle is essential even for pre-retirement owners.

Here are a few examples of Pinnacle statements from large companies:

- "Become a one stop-shop for clean energy."[24] (Electric car, Solar Roof, and Power Wall home battery.) —Tesla

- "To fuel a 'biotech machine' that will create drugs to treat your genetically predisposed diseases."[25]—23andMe

- "Getting a million tons [of cargo] to the surface of Mars and creating a self-sustaining city."[26] —SpaceX

- "To be the most influential storyteller of a new Africa."[27] —EbonyLife TV

- "Making the best product matters for saving the planet."[28] —Patagonia

You can find your Pinnacle by thinking about what your company would look like with a 5–50X impact. As discussed at the beginning of the book, your company can 5X its value in five years by growing revenues 20 percent per annum while doubling its profit margin.

In comparison, 50X-ing your business is ambitious and might take you 20 years to achieve, although one of Greg's clients, Discover Strength, grew its value by approximately 250X over a seven-year period (more about their story in The Climb chapter later in the book).

To grow that fast, you may need to enter new markets and acquire and fund new businesses, as Amazon and Google have done.

Here are the Pinnacle statements of some of our clients:

- "1,000,000 net-zero homes created." —Atlas Home Energy Solutions

- "Saving 10,000,000 hours per year." —Adriana Accounting

- "10,000 users under management." —Reliable Technologies

- "E3: Exceptional Experience for Everyone." —BankVista

- "Early Detection Allows You to Live with Confidence." —Veravas (antibody detection)

- "100 locations with 100 million dollars in revenue." —Discover Strength

Your Medium-term Milestones

Now, project yourself three to five years into the future. It is December 31, and you are walking through your business. What does it look like?

What profit and revenue did you achieve this year? What progress did you make toward your Pinnacle? What does your team look like at the leadership level and beyond? How systemized is your business? What strategic relationships have you built with your customers and parallel vendors? What does your physical infrastructure look like? How is your thought leadership progressing?

Your subconscious mind does not differentiate between vision and reality, and you can condition it to move you toward a strong vision that you imagine. Top athletes have used this approach for decades to normalize in their minds the moments of athletic glory in advance, so that they can naturally manifest it when the time comes.

You can do the same for your business. Condition yourself and your team to make your Medium-term Milestones a reality by frequently envisioning it. Medium-term Milestones help everyone in the company understand where you are going together and feel more informed for making day-to-day decisions. (See Figure 4.2.)

Figure 4.2: Medium-term Milestones example

Target Date:	12/31/202X
Profit:	$ 1,500,000
Revenue:	$ 11,000,000
Profit/Employee:	$ 16,667
Other Key Metric:	150 Net Zero Houses

- 90 Employees / 25 Install Trucks
- Branded & productised services
- 25% market share in PA
- HR & IT functions on Leadership Team
- N-Z House Monitoring service offered
- Mastered HVAC and Solar
- Defined and ingrained core processes
- $ 6.0 M Duct Revenue
- $ 3.5 M HVAC Revenue
- $ 1.5 M Solar / $ 0.2 M Audit Revenue

Formulate your Medium-term Milestones with broad strokes, focusing on the major accomplishments you want to achieve by the end of three years, or five years. Start with revenue and follow with profit. We like to do this by looking at the current net profit margin of the business and assuming that it would be gradually improved.

It is highly unlikely that you would be able to jump from 3 percent profitability to 20 percent in one year unless you have grossly underpriced your products and services. It is more realistic to imagine that by systemizing your business, you would harvest economies over time, and by differentiating your offering, you would be able to raise prices. Profit improvement is a process, and moving from 3 percent to 12–15 percent can be realistic over a three-year period, but not overnight.

Pick a metric that demonstrates your progress toward your Pinnacle. In the earlier mentioned examples, our clients targeted metrics in their Pinnacle such as "10,000 users under management," "100 right people in the right seats," and "1,000,000 net-zero houses." If you do the same, where will your company be on the metrics you've picked in three years' time?

Ideally, you would be on your way toward your Pinnacle. We like to calculate the year-on-year growth toward our clients' Pinnacles using an individual metric or the client's Pinnacle revenue target and applying that over three years to see whether the business would be growing proportionately.

But this does not always work because some companies factor in future acquisitions that stair-step them toward their Pinnacle in later years, while allowing them to slow-walk their growth in the nearer term.

The great benefit of your Medium-term Milestones is that they help you formulate a rock-solid One-Year Growth Plan. More on this in Mountain Four: Perform.

Key Ideas from Practice 4: Vision

- To create a vision, start by unearthing your Why: why your organization exists beyond making money for shareholders, supplying employees with a paycheck, and delivering products or services.

- Pick a long-term energizing goal that furthers your Why and makes it measurable. This is the Pinnacle of your business.

- Paint full-color Medium-term Milestones for your company three to five years out, en route to your Pinnacle so that your team can share a mental image of the organization's future. This helps you share your vision with everyone in the organization, so that your team can help you make it a reality.

Now that you have a compelling vision, it's time to figure out the strategy that will help you get there.

PRACTICE 5: STRATEGY

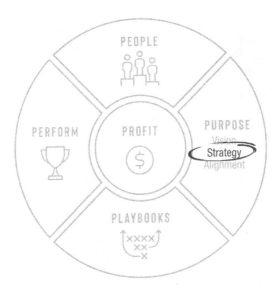

"More businesses die of indigestion than starvation."

—Bill Hewlett

Strategy helps you determine how you will make your Medium-term Milestones reality. It is your game plan that will help you grow your business in a profitable and systematic manner, notwithstanding competition and changes in the economy.

There are two approaches to the Strategy Principle we consider first. One of them involves positioning your organization by determining your core business, ideal customers, your brand promises, and how you prove them. The other concept looks at differentiating your company in the eyes of your ideal customers so that you can charge prices that allow for sufficient profitability to grow.

We apply these concepts with the help of a Pinnacle tool we call Strategy Squares. (See Figure 5.1.) It was inspired by Verne Harnish's "7 Strata of Strategy"[29] and *Harvard Business Review*'s On Strategy.[30]

Figure 5.1: Strategy Squares

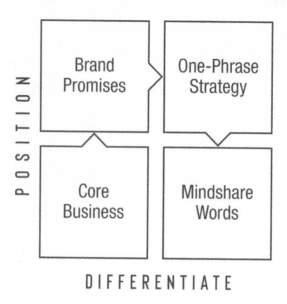

DIFFERENTIATE

First, how do you position your business by starting from your Core Business and Ideal Customers to find your Brand Promises?

Then, how do you express your Strategy succinctly, so that each of your people gets exactly what you are about?

Finally, can you manifest your strategy by finding or coining differentiating words and expressions that will make your business memorable for your ideal customers?

Your Core Business

Most small businesses make the mistake of trying to be all things to all people. This is natural, because often the business started with the owner providing products and services based on their personal expertise for their business connections.

This is the phenomenon Michael Gerber, author of *The E-Myth*, refers to as "technicians starting businesses." Initially, technicians sell their capabilities to whomever will pay as a way to replace the income from a job they left.

When Steve started his consulting business, his initial goal was to replace his previous salary from a banking job. His take-home pay was $4,000 a month at the time, and he figured that if he could bill the same amount as a business, it would maintain his family's lifestyle. He could then evolve the business from there.

This initial goal prompted him to take on any business he could figure out how to deliver. These included raising investments for a fledgling venture capital fund, preparing a discounted cash flow valuation model for an entrepreneur restructuring his business, and advising on a management buyout.

As he got busier, it dawned on Steve that this business model was completely unscalable. He could hardly figure out how to deliver all these services himself, let alone delegating anything to others.

Shortly thereafter, a government-owned development bank started a capital investment program for small businesses, and Steve began to offer business owners a service to take advantage of this opportunity. This was a business process that, if successful, could be repeated, systemized, and delegated. As soon as he won the first such mandate, he documented the steps and taught a young graduate to help him with execution.

Over the next couple of years, Steve built a small team to deliver this capital-raising consulting service. Later, that business became commoditized, and they moved on to offering strategic business sale preparation and execution services. That became their core business, where they found enough opportunities to grow, while staying in a narrow enough field to create systemized processes.

Steve then hired and trained smart young graduates to execute the technical part of their services, such as writing offering memoranda and building financial projection models. These graduates were attracted to an intellectually challenging and varied job and could be hired at a reasonable cost, which allowed the business to become profitable and scalable.

As you can see, finding the right niche for this business allowed it to flourish. A still bigger benefit in narrowing your business's target market is that it creates constraints for the company to push against.

Constraints define the boundaries of your domain and stimulate your creativity, akin to how a river speeds up in a gorge: As the water is squeezed into a narrow passage, its energy multiplies.

You can then harvest that energy to come up with new product offerings and marketing ideas.

Your Ideal Customer

Who are your ideal customers that benefit the most from your products or services? Ideal customers may be individual consumers or businesses, depending on the type of product you offer.

If you are selling to businesses, what geography do you target? If you are a mom-and-pop shop or a franchisee, it may be your neighborhood. In contrast, a managed service provider likely serves businesses in a 100-mile radius. A corporate law firm may work statewide or beyond, and a software business may target a global audience.

For example, Media Cybernetics, mentioned earlier, is a small business with clients situated across four continents who are served through a global dealer network and a self-service digital portal.

Having defined your geographic footprint, let's determine the types of businesses you serve. What industries do they operate in, and what size are they? Are you selling to the corporate headquarters or to their local branch or office?

Within these businesses, which people do you target? In small businesses, decisions are likely made at the top by the CEO or owner. If you target larger companies or public entities, your buyers may be at the middle management or C-suite level. What are the positions of the people you need to talk to and engage to make a sale? How do you reach them?

If you are selling direct to consumers, where do these people congregate? They may be on LinkedIn or Facebook, Instagram, etc. Figure out where you meet them.

For virtual service businesses, psychographics are more important than geographics and demographics. The mindset of your ideal customers—how they think, how they buy, what's important to them—is often best expressed by creating avatars for them.

Luke Carlson, Founder and CEO of Discover Strength, talks about two personas that make up 70 percent of the company's "Ideal Customers."

Mary: 45 years old; professional; attorney; $220,000 income; looks good but wants to shed 10 lbs. and look better; spins; wine drinker; enjoys getaways to South Beach; regular Med Spa treatments; shops at Lululemon and Nordstrom; involved in charity/philanthropy; loves a challenge; likes her life "scheduled."

Michael: 56 years old; executive; $275,000 income; wine and whiskey drinker; golfs; Colorado ski trips; a couple of adult children; full schedule; values his time; Type A; wears a sport coat and great shoes.

Your Brand Promises

Having figured out your core business and who your Ideal Customers are, it's time to articulate the compelling benefits of becoming a customer of your business. Your brand promises are concise and credible commitments that your business can deliver on consistently.

Here are a few examples from iconic companies:

- Amazon: "Broadest selection, lowest prices, minimal hassle."[31]

- 23andMe: "Actionable health insights, ancestry, traits."[32]

- Coca-Cola: "To inspire moments of optimism and uplift."[33]

- BMW: "The ultimate driving machine."[34]

- Patagonia: "Build products that last for generations or can be recycled so the materials in them remain in use."[35]

- ActOne: "Successful Resolutions for Complex Situations."[36]

And sample brand promises from a handful of our Pinnacle clients:

- Groove Commerce (e-commerce agency): "Follow a growth mindset, set revenue goals and deliver clear paths to reach them."

- LookThink (digital experience design and development): "Impactful platforms, Compelling digital brands."

- Adriana Accounting (bank-accounting software): "Easy to learn, high ROI, we help you."

- Atlas Home Energy Solutions (energy efficiency contracting): "Lower utility bills, increased comfort, fresher air."

- BankVista (community bank): "Highly personalized, responsive and flexible, committed to community."

- Gardner Builders (general contractor): "Great relationships with design partners, owners and project managers."

It's great to come up with compelling brand promises, but how do you prove them to your customers? We call these proof metrics "Kept Promise Indicators" (KPIs). If you can't prove how you deliver on your brand promises, then you may not actually be delivering.

One of Atlas Home Energy Solutions' brand promises is to lower energy usage. Atlas can prove this by analyzing the utility bills of their customers and showing the reduction as a result of energy-efficiency improvements.

Another AHES brand promise is increased comfort in the home. The company can prove that it delivers on this promise with its 4.9-star rating and 350 rave reviews on Google. The AHES Experience is backed up by hundreds of testimonials from happy customers.

Your One-Phrase Strategy

"If you can't explain it, you don't understand it well enough."

—Albert Einstein

Coming up with a powerful differentiating strategy is hard. What is even harder is explaining it to your frontline employees so that they can make day-to-day decisions to execute it.

Here is where the "one-phrase strategy" comes in. "You're better off with a strategy that is 80% right and 100% implemented than [having] one that is 100% right but doesn't drive consistent action throughout the company."[37]

IKEA built a business on the idea of the "Flat Pack" by creating simple and practical furniture that can be stored in small places, fits into a passenger car, and can be assembled by the customer.[38]

Starbucks built its business on the idea of becoming "The Third Place" between customers' home and office.[39] Regulars can swing by in the morning to pick up a drink while listening to mellow tunes, relax with a book, or work on their computer in a cozy environment. The baristas are nice and friendly and will replace customers' drinks if they're not fully satisfied.

Southwest Airlines built a consistently growing and highly profitable business in a "red ocean" industry on the basis of the idea of "Wheels Up." Southwest realized that what people want is low fares, availability, and reliability and that they would be happy to give up taken-for-granted food services and assigned seating on short flights. This allowed the airline to reengineer its offering and become both attractive to low-budget travelers and highly profitable.

"Wheels Up" expresses to all Southwest employees that their job is to keep their most valuable assets in the air as much as possible. According to Tableu, a subsidiary of data software giant Salesforce, seven hundred Southwest planes fly on average 5.7 routes a day,[40] compared to the global average of 4.5[41]—a much lower daily routes number even though other airlines have been trying to copy Southwest's practices for years. Upon taking the helm of GE in 1981, Jack Welch launched its strategy of "Number One, Number Two, or Get Out." During his twenty-year leadership, GE increased its market cap from $14 billion to $410 billion.[42]

It's not just fortune companies that can come up with simple, powerfully differentiating strategies. Here are a few examples from Pinnacle client businesses:

- Atlas Home Energy Solutions: "Hit It Hard"

- GERSTEL, Inc. (distributor of precision instruments): "First to Be Called"

- Groove Commerce (e-commerce consultants): "We grow when our clients grow"

- Media Cybernetics (imaging software developer): "Imaging Lab Ecosystem"

- OST Global Solutions (helps win government contracts): "Keep Adding Value"

- Genz Ryan HVAC (diagnose and fix it without return visits) "One Trip"

Your Mindshare Words

What are the words that you "own" in the minds of your customers? Most businesses miss a huge opportunity by not branding their products and services, which then never leave the default positioning of being a commodity.

What power do branding words and phrases wield?

Consider Starbucks, which staked out a category of one as a coffee shop. Starbucks managed to brand one of the oldest and most commoditized food services: selling coffee. How did it do that?

Starbucks created a distinctive experience and branded every element of it. They have drinks like Starbucks Reserve, Pike Place, Lightnote Blend, Ready Brew, Beach Bellini, and Raspberry Riot. They even branded their servers Baristas, and their cup sizes Tall and Venti.

Arguably, Starbucks does not serve the best coffee, but it is one of the most expensive coffee experiences. Starbucks coffee shops are everywhere, and the company has grown to dominate the coffee business on main streets and in malls, hotels, and supermarkets.

Another example is Apple, which created distinctive product brands like the iPhone, the iPad, and the iMac—these are Apple's branded equivalents of the cell phone, tablet, and personal computer sold by competitors. Branded brick-and-mortar Apple Stores offer to freely troubleshoot products for customers in their Genius Bar.

Branding your employees is a powerful and fun opportunity to bolster the identity of your team members, who are working for a great and cohesive company. Here are a few examples:

- Groove Commerce: "Groovers"

- Virid: "Viridians"

- Optimal Networks: "Optimalites"

- Ogburn Construction: "Ogies"

- Media Minefield: "Miners"

Figure 5.2 Pinnacle Pyramid Part 2: Strategy

Key Ideas from Practice 5: Strategy

- Your strategy is how you will accomplish your vision. It includes how you position and how you differentiate your business in the marketplace.

- Start by defining your core business and your ideal customers. You can't be all things to all people.

- Discover your brand promises. What can you do better and differently from others that makes your ideal customers choose your company? Articulate your kept promise indicators (KPIs) that prove you are delivering on your Brand Promises.

- Operationalize your Strategy by distilling it into a short, pithy phrase that all your employees can understand and act upon.

- Find and develop words you can own in the minds of your customers, so eventually you will be seen as head and shoulders above your undifferentiated competitors.

Your vision and strategy are only valuable when you align your organization around them. More on that next.

PRACTICE 6: ALIGNMENT

"Building a visionary company is 1 percent vision and 99 percent alignment. When you have superb alignment, a visitor could drop in from outer space and infer your vision from the operations and activities of the company without ever reading it on paper or meeting a single senior executive."

—Jim Collins

It is easy to have a vision—everyone has one. True, some of us are more vision-oriented than others, and we all have different interests and abilities when it comes to looking ahead. Dan Sullivan of Strategic Coach advocates developing a 25 year personal vision. Others look ahead only for the next year or the next quarter.

There is a correlation between the length of your vision and your earning power. An hourly worker's vision often focuses on the next hour or the day ahead. A supervisor has to have a view of the upcoming week. A midlevel manager will have a vision for the next month. A C-level executive must see into the coming quarter, and the CEO, a year or more ahead.

A president or prime minister has to have a vision of at least four years, until the next election, but a skilled statesman or woman should look even further ahead. Winston Churchill invoked a vision of the fate of the British Empire that allowed him to inspire his citizens to prepare themselves for years of valiant struggle.

Alignment is about harmonizing visions. It is about using regular *Reinforcement* for getting everybody on the same page in understanding where the company is going and how it is planning to get there.

It is also about *Integrating* your Vision and Strategy into a coherent ideology, which is than weaved into everything you do.

Figure 6.1 Alignment Accelerators

By giving your people a longer-term vision, you help them put their own work in context. Vision allows them to see how their often menial or apparently trivial efforts contribute to building a great company and achieving a noble purpose.

By painting and socializing your vision, you put all your people center stage in a great saga. You build their pride in being part of an amazing community and playing a role in changing the world.

Just don't expect people to get your vision immediately. For many, long-term thinking is an alien domain. It will take months and possibly years of exposure for these ideas to take root in the thinking of every employee in your business.

In *Built to Last*, Jim Collins and Jerry Porras talk about alignment as being a practice rather than a one-time act. It takes months and years for everybody to align around your vision and strategy by gradually internalizing them. Beyond the time they need to really understand each of the concepts, employees will also have to buy into the plan.

The first step in creating alignment is regularly Reinforcing your company's vision, strategy, and strategic plan.

The tool for doing that is a two-page business plan called—you guessed it—the Strategic Vision and Execution Plan (SVEP). (See Figure 6.2.) Share the SVEP with your employees regularly, at least once a quarter. Be prepared to revisit and reinforce the plan quarter after quarter, as it will take a couple of years for it to fully sink in and for your people to internalize it.

Figure 6.2: Strategic Vision and Execution Plan

THE STRATEGIC VISION & EXECUTION PLAN

PURPOSE: WHY WE EXIST?	PINNACLE: THE TOP OF OUR MOUNTAIN	ANNUAL GROWTH PLAN	
		Target date:	
		Profit:	
		Revenue:	
		Profit/Employee:	
		Key Metric:	

CORE BUSINESS	MEDIUM TERM MILESTONES		Goals
	Target date:		**1**
	Profit:		
	Revenue:		
	Profit/Employee:		**2**
	Key Metric:		
	•		**3**
	•		
	•		
CORE VALUES To Live Values & Purpose	•		**4**
	•		
	•		**5**
	•		
	•		
	•		**6**
	•		
	•		**7**
	•		

TRENDS

1. _____   4. _____

2. _____   5. _____

3. _____   6. _____

STRATEGIC VISION & EXECUTION PLAN: PAGE 2

QUARTERLY EXECUTION		QUARTERLY THEME

Target date:		Theme Name
Profit:		
Revenue:		
Profit/Employee:		Celebration / Reward.
Key Metric:		

Rocks	**Flywheel Design**
	Describe and/or sketch your design in this space

Rocks	
1	
2	
3	
4	

One Phrase Strategy

5	
6	

	Brand Promises	Brand Promise KPIs
7	1	
	2	
8	3	
	4	
9	5	

STRENGTHS/CORE COMPETENCIES

1. _____
2. _____
3. _____

WEAKNESSES

1. _____
2. _____
3. _____

The employees who get it will be excited and will bring their energy to the quest. Others may not be interested in what you are trying to do. Don't try to convert them. Let them go and find the company or community where they belong. Your business's purpose is not for everyone.

Develop and Integrate Your Ideology

Socializing your strategic vision and execution plan is just the first step. In order to create the alignment of a "visionary company," you need to go much deeper than that. You have to *Integrate* what Jim Collins calls your "core ideology" into everything you do as a company.

The best way to build your ideology is to look at your Culture as defined by your core values, your Why, and your Pinnacle. How can you manifest your behaviors, attitudes, beliefs, and long-term goals into your strategies, goals, tactics, policies, processes, company traditions, the name of your people, office layouts, job designs, incentive schemes, and so forth?

Jim Collins gives examples of how Ford implemented its ideology to improve its quality across departments, employee engagement programs, supplier selection, management practices, internal communications infrastructure, agreements with unions, customer feedback processes, and company awards.[43]

Another example Collins gives is Merck, the pharmaceutical company that aligned its business around its Why of "benefitting humanity through innovative contributions to medicine." Merck subordinated its profit motive to driving its ideology. As a result, the company built research laboratories with academic atmospheres and appearance to attract prominent scientists.

These scientists were encouraged to collaborate with top universities and often received promotions to high-paying positions without having to take on management roles. Instead of playing it safe by keeping many irons in the product development fire, the company placed outsized bets on producing breakthrough drugs that would surpass competitors' offerings.

Collins also writes about Hewlett Packard (HP), the founders of which stipulated that the company must make its profits through significant technical contributions. This ideology led to HP hiring only the top 10 percent of graduates from prestigious engineering schools like the Massachusetts Institute of Technology (MIT) and Stanford.

The company also resisted jumping on the IBM-clone bandwagon when the personal computer market was set to explode. Unless it could substantially reinvent the PC, it wouldn't go down that path. If there were no significant technical contributions to make, that was not a business HP would be in.

It's all well and good for fortune companies to develop ideologies, but how can a smaller, private company afford to do it?

Let's see a couple of examples.

Alignment Example 1

We earlier talked about Atlas Home Energy Solutions (AHES), a home energy efficiency contractor. Let's look at its core ideology, which is based on its core values, Why, and Pinnacle.

AHES's core values are as follows:

o   Takes Pride in Their Work

o   Selflessly Supports the Team

o   Treats Customers with Respect

AHES's Why: "To advance life at home"

AHES's Pinnacle: "1,000,000 net-zero homes created by 2040"

Now, let's see some examples of what AHES has done to integrate its core ideology:

Strategy: Design and train the team on a process that converts homes to net-zero quickly and with high quality.

Alignment impacts: Proud employees, consistent execution, better quality of life in the home for the customer.

Tactic: Design a metric to measure energy use of a prospective customer's house. Demonstrate needed combination of energy savings and renewable energy generation tactics to cover the gap.

Alignment impacts: Makes service tangible and attractive. Advances life at home by making owners environmentally responsible. Proud employees. Consistent execution. New net-zero houses created.

Goal: Create 100 net-zero homes in 2024.

Alignment impacts: Selfless support to the team is required to execute stretch goal. Advancing life. Working for a company that contributes to meaningful change makes employees proud.

Policy: Only take on customers where a net-zero impact is achievable.

Alignment impacts: Advancing life in homes by only working with environmentally responsible customers. Employee pride. All efforts focused on creating net-zero homes. Net zero is only achieved by working as a team that selflessly supports each other.

Company traditions: Ringing the bell for each new net-zero home sale and completion. Net-zero jacket worn by employee of the month. Net-zero dinner for top 50 customers whose house achieved the largest "plus over net-zero" impact.

Office layout: Net-zero office building with demonstrations of all energy-saving and renewable energy generation tactics employed by the company: insulation materials, heat pumps, solar panels, battery wall, electric trucks used by employees, etc.

Job designs: Salesperson: Net-Zero Developer; Project staff: Net-Zero Builder; Office staff: Net-Zero Facilitator

Alignment implications: All the core values, the Why, and the Pinnacle are manifested.

Can you now see how reinforcing and integrating your culture vision and strategy can have your people row in the same direction?

Figure 6.3: Rowing in the same direction

Alignment Example 2

Media Cybernetics is an imaging software developer. Below are the elements of its core ideology:

Media Cybernetics' core values:

- Problem Solver

- Team Oriented

- Acts with a Sense of Ownership

- Passionate about the Customer Experience

- Open and Honest

Media Cybernetic's Why: To advance innovation in partnership with the scientific community.

Media Cybernetic's Pinnacle: To become the world's most user-centric scientific imaging ecosystem.

Strategy: Imaging Lab Ecosystem

Alignment implications: Must win over imaging community, work as a team to deliver superior product and customer experience, employees must take ownership of problems to move fast and work as a team to solve them.

Tactic: Build vibrant community of student users.

Alignment implications: Solves the problem of access for early-career users, who will generate a community and content to improve customer experience. Builds partnership with the scientific community. Solves the problem of students not having the budget to purchase the software. Community and content co-creation generates ownership and user-centeredness.

Policy: Annual version releases

Alignment implications: Release discipline forces company to innovate continually. New releases keep improving customer experience. Release schedule requires intense teamwork and problem solving. Partnership with scientific user community provides feedback in beta testing.

Office layout: Virtual operations with team members and strategic partners in United States, Canada, Europe, and Asia

Alignment implications: True global native company leveraging cultural and product design feedback through different regions and ethnicities. Creates user centricity and engages employees globally, who feel ownership of the geographically distributed organization.

There are many more examples. The core ideology for the practice of Alignment in the business is a never-ending quest of creating a unique and inspired culture.

It took Truett Cathy, Chick-Fil-A's founder, years to get the response "My Pleasure" adopted throughout his fast-food chain.[44]

It will take a couple of years, or longer, but with persistence, focus, and creativity, you can build a visionary company staffed with A-Players and A-Potentials who are deeply passionate and proud of your business. You will have a business of missionaries who want what you want. They will be your nation, and together you will take your business to the Pinnacle.

Key Ideas from Practice 6: Alignment

- Start by regularly—at least quarterly—reinforcing your core values, vision, and strategy by sharing them with your team.

- Develop an ideology for your business that is based on your company's core values, the Why, and the Pinnacle.

- Integrate your ideology into the fabric of your business by weaving it into every strategy, tactic, goal, policy, and even your office layout, job designs, and job title.

Messages from Mountain Two: Purpose

The second Pinnacle Principle is Purpose, and it includes the Pinnacle Practices of Vision, Strategy, and Alignment.

Your company's **Vision** includes its reason for existing, or your Why, which could remain unchanged for 100 years; your long-term energizing goal called the Pinnacle; and Medium-term Milestones, which allow your employees to see the future company through your eyes.

Your **Strategy** includes definition of your core business and ideal customers, and how your business differentiates itself by expressing your brand promises, one-phrase strategy, and mindshare words.

Your vision is irrelevant unless everyone in the business understands and supports it. You can build a visionary company by regularly discussing your Strategic Vision and Execution Plan with your employees and by integrating your core values, Why, and Pinnacle into the fabric of your company.

By focusing on **aligning** everyone with your company's ideology, you can build a business full of A-Players and A-Potentials who share your beliefs and work as missionaries to achieve your vision.

Now that you have defined your Culture and Functions and are Coaching your People, your Purpose is the fuel for the motor of your business. You provide the sparks to the engine as it accelerates your momentum.

The next step is to systemize your best practices to allow delegation and consistent and flawless execution of your unique way of doing business. That requires Playbooks, which we talk about in the next chapter.

MOUNTAIN THREE: PLAYBOOKS

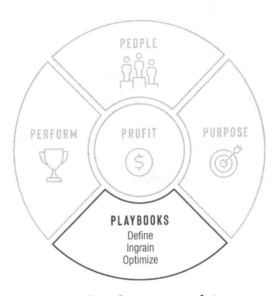

"If you can't describe what you are doing as a process, you don't know what you are doing."

—Edward Deming

In late 2004, after celebrating the second birthday of his firm, MB Partners, Steve suffered a giant blow that eventually turned out to be a blessing in disguise.

We spoke earlier about the equity investment program that a government owned development bank had launched 18 months earlier. MB Partners was one of the first firms to embrace it and carved out a leading role in helping clients use it to their best advantage. The person who ran that department at the bank was apparently irritated by MB Partners' success, and he instructed his teams to no longer process any projects that Steve's firm sponsored.

At the time, these projects represented 90 percent of their business, and MB Partners had four people on staff, with a growing overhead. They had to reinvent themselves immediately and find a new revenue source, or they would be soon out of business.

Steve and his colleagues then turned their attention to seeking engagements from small business owners who wanted to sell their businesses to strategic or private equity buyers. Trouble was, they had zero experience with such deals. Thankfully, Steve had friends in a regional mergers and acquisitions (M&A) network that MB Partners had cofounded a year earlier who could teach them how to do M&A deals.

Steve learned that selling a business required the production of a selling memorandum about the company and the creation of an elaborate business plan with a complex financial projection that enabled investors to study the prospects of the business and ascertain its value.

The challenge was that it apparently took two to three months to produce these documents for a monthly retainer paid by the client. Steve realized that they could only cover their overhead if they cut production time down to three weeks and take the three months' retainer upfront.

This was Steve's initiation to systemizing his business. They had to create a process to produce these documents with a team of medium-level and junior employees. They ended up modularizing the selling memo and the financial model in order to delegate the mechanical parts to analysts and the problem-solving modules to vice presidents. They created a memorandum factory that allowed them to break even at the front end, with selling commissions generating their profits.

As a happy byproduct of systemization, the quality of MB Partners' memos went way up thanks to developing a consistent formula for research and organization. Clients were delighted with going to market within four weeks rather than in three months, that competitors were offering. MB

Partners grew rapidly from that point onward.

The reason so many companies fail to scale is that they can't get their Playbooks down on paper. Franchises are sold because they have a playbook for everything. Think McDonalds' Hamburger University. It's not about cooking hamburgers; it's about running a business where 15 year-olds work alongside 50 year-olds and where a restaurant can turn a predictable profit even when staff turns over three times a year.

Greg talks about systemizing your business as your opportunity to create your own "Payroll Protection Program" (PPP) for your business. Better than waiting for the US government to disburse funds to save your company, as it did during the 2020–21 pandemic.

Pinnacle's "PPP" acronym stands for Playbooks taking Pressure off People. Creating blueprints of your best practices will empower your team to execute with curiosity, consistency, and confidence.

PRACTICE 7: DEFINE

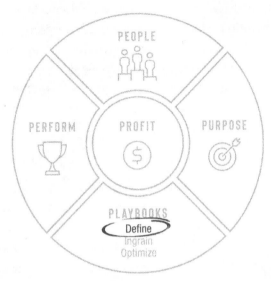

"Systemize the predictable and humanize everything else."

—Isadore Sharp

The bottleneck is always at the top of the bottle. A business can only grow to the extent that its leadership evolves in impact and productivity. Leadership teams grow to the degree that they delegate and focus on higher-leverage activities, such as leading and strategically growing their respective functions.

The visionary leader of a business should eventually delegate running the company to a skilled Second in Command (2IC) in order to focus on creating alignment around the vision and strategy, integrating the core ideology through the business, building the brand, finding growth opportunities, nurturing big relationships, making acquisitions, and being the ambassador for their company.

Visionaries as well as 2ICs should gradually delegate all functional activities and focus on leading and coaching their functional leaders, facilitating problem solving, making decisions, removing obstacles from functional leaders' way, and making and achieving business plans.

The functional leaders themselves should endeavor, over time, to delegate all execution-related activities in their respective functions, and focus on leadership and management activities. They must make sure their direct reports are delivering the outcomes defined for their respective subfunctions, achieving their Rocks, hitting their metrics, and exhibiting the core values of the company.

The less *doing* the leadership team members do, the more they can lead, solve problems, and foster the culture of ownership and accountability.

Successful delegation requires repeatable systems and processes. Your direct reports are by definition less experienced and, most likely, less intuitive than you are. They have to rely on blueprints to deliver a comparable quality output that *you* can do based on your years of experience and honed judgment. They need Playbooks to follow. (We use *playbook* and *process* as interchangeable synonyms in this book.)

The Playbooks You Need

In 2005, Steve read Michael Gerber's *The E-Myth Revisited* and decided to document the processes of his advisory business. The only example he had in front of him was an ISO 9001 manual, which was over 300 pages long. He started creating a highly detailed blueprint for the company but soon realized that the effort was futile. It required so much minutia to document that it would have taken weeks to complete, and result in a manual already out of date.

Then, he remembered that the bank he used to work for had a similar problem. As the secretary of the executive board, Steve witnessed how board members spent 30 percent of their time reviewing and approving processes. These were 50 to 70 page documents produced by a 15 strong Organization Department.

The bank had about 400 documented processes, each of which had to be updated every two years. Consequently, every week, three to five of these thick, stapled drafts were presented to the board for approval.

Of course, the directors wouldn't spend hours scrutinizing detailed procedures, which they did not need to know in the first place. They duly rubber-stamped these tomes, which went back into the drawer and few people would ever read them.

This type of process is not what we have in mind for the **Define** Practice. Your goal is to create a "company bible" that contains the critical Playbooks of your business.

The goal is not to micromanage smart and competent people. It is to document your company's way of doing business so that you create consistency around best practices ,and can onboard new employees with a clear description of your operating system. By documenting your Playbooks, you create a repeatable baseline description of your key operations that can be refined over time. Without having best practices documented, you have nothing to measure against and improve.

As the organization grows, your processes will need to become more detailed. You can achieve this by building out deeper levels of process below your existing Playbooks, by creating simple checklists, and by shooting videos of the right and best ways of doing things.

Playbooks, Procedures, and Policies

A **playbook** is a high-level, linear, bullet-pointed description of the main steps of executing a critical process in your business. Think of it as the floorplan of a room in a house.

A statement of procedures, abbreviated as **SOP**, is a detailed, step-by-step description of a series of tasks, something like the architectural drawings for the room, with all the nooks and crannies laid out with exact measurements so that the builder can construct them without further instruction.

Policies describe principles and courses of action adopted by an organization. For example, the vacation policy governs how many leave days employees can take and how they can book these days without disrupting the operation of the business. Think of policies as the construction regulations governing how houses can be built in a certain location.

The Benefits of Defining Your Playbooks

The low-hanging fruit of systemizing a small business is to define a baseline set of processes that can be documented and communicated quickly and in simple terms.

Creating Playbooks catalyzes dramatic improvements in several areas of your company:

1. Your Playbooks, taken together, give you a concise operating manual for your business. You can hand this to new employees, and they will immediately understand how your business works and how they can contribute from day one.

2. You will have documented the best practices of your company, so the playbook gives you a blueprint of the best way of running critical parts of your business. This is a potent tool to drive consistency and accountability going forward.

3. Your Playbooks represent a baseline upon which future improvements can be made. You can start scoreboarding the quality and frequency of execution and look for ways to simplify your Playbooks and drive improvements in efficiency, quality, and customer experience.

4. By defining your Playbooks you can ultimately eliminate any single-person dependency in your business and become truly scalable.

Five Steps for Defining Playbooks

Figure 7.1: Five Steps for Creating Playbooks

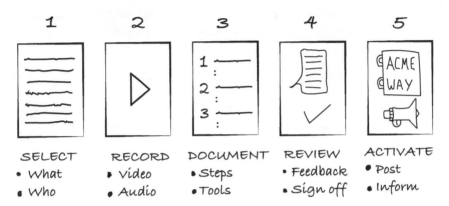

Source: Design inspired by the work of David Jenyns.

Step 1: Select Your Critical Playbooks

So, what are the main Playbooks that drive your business?

The Get Work, Do Work, and Get Paid framework is a good place to start.

Getting Work requires Playbooks for marketing and sales.

Doing Work could necessitate, depending on the type of business, the following Playbooks: client onboarding, account management, project delivery, professional services, software development, quality assurance, and customer service, etc.

Getting Paid could require Playbooks for areas like finance, accounting, people, office management, procurement, and payroll, etc.

What is your company's way of creating value? What are your best practices that need to be made consistent across the business? Pick the Playbooks that are essential to run your organization. We have seen companies initially select between six and fifteen Playbooks to document.

Eventually, you should document Playbooks for every area of your business that has repetitive processes and eliminate any single person dependency in your company.

So where should you start? Your most important assets are your people and your clients. Start by defining the journey you want them to experience when coming into contact with your business.

The Pinnacle Playbooks Starting kit includes two Playbooks:

1. The Employee Journey Playbook, which documents how we attract, hire, onboard, and help employees be successful in your business

Figure 7.2: Employee Journey Playbook

EMPLOYEE JOURNEY

- DEFINE FUNCTION
- ADVERTISE POSITION
- APPLICATIONS
- TESTING
- INTERVIEWS
- OFFER
- WELCOME GIFT
- WELCOME DAY
- ONBOARDING
- DEFINE EXPECTATIONS
- TRAINING AND DEVELOPMENT
- MENTOR MEETINGS
- ANNUAL REVIEW & PLAN
- PROMOTIONS
- OFFBOARDING

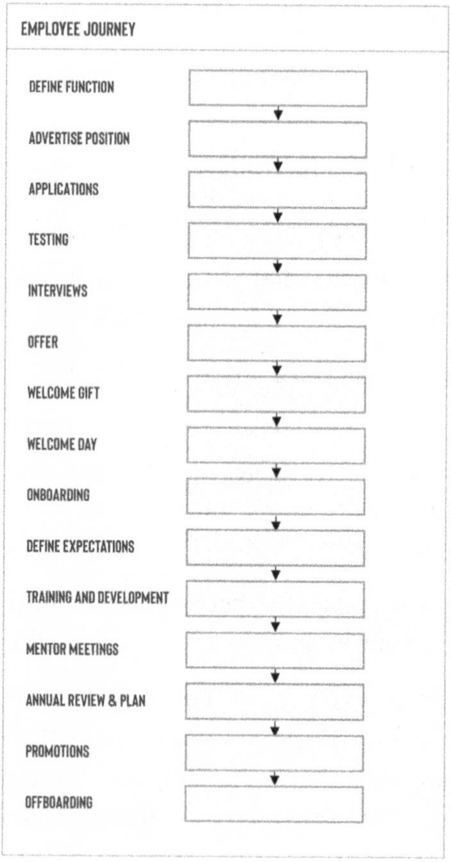

Source: Inspired by David Jenyn's: Systemology

2. The Customer Journey Playbook is a process for your customers. How do they find you, become a customer, and how do you help them succeed, grow, become an evergreen client that refer you prospects and might even become a strategic partner for your business?

Figure 7.3: Customer Journey Playbook

CUSTOMER JOURNEY

CREATE CONTENT	
CAPTURE LEAD	
NURTURE	
CLOSE SALE	
BILLING	
ONBOARD	
MAKE SUCCESSFUL	
MAKE RECURRING	
GROW REVENUES	
GET REFERRALS	
BUILD PARTNERSHIP	

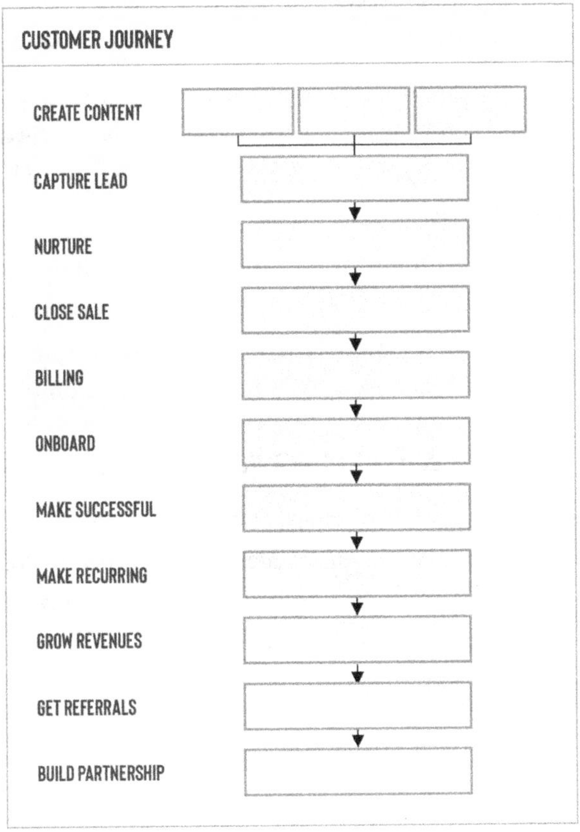

Source: Inspired by David Jenyn's: Systemology

These Playbooks will help you attract great people and to start eliminating single-person dependencies in the process of making money in your business.

Step 2: Record on Video or Audio

Have an employee whose performance represents the best practice in your organization perform the process and record it using the most frictionless method. You can use screen recording software, video, or a voice recording app.

Out in the field, a GoPro camera may be the most practical. In a sales situation, recording the audio with your phone is the least distracting for the salesperson.

This is the most convenient form for the person eventually documenting the playbook, because they can take as long as they need without the process-performer present.

If you are documenting your own playbook, recording audio or video allows you to have some distance between doing and observing the process, which may include some intuitive details that you do not notice while performing and would miss in straight textual description.

Step 3: Document Your Playbooks

When documenting your Playbooks, stay at a high level. A good rule of thumb is the Pareto principle, which states that for many outcomes, roughly 80 percent of consequences come from 20 percent of causes[45]. Accordingly, focus on documenting the 20 percent of the process that most likely delivers 80 percent of the results.

Try to fit the documentation of each process on one or two pages. Restrict your Playbooks to the most important linear steps. Including six to ten steps is typical.

Then, describe each step with two to seven bullet points. Who is doing what and with which tools? Don't micromanage the steps. Remember, you are not writing an SOP here. You can fill in the details later, if you need to, with simple checklists, videos, and so forth.

By keeping Playbooks at a high level, you make them more enduring, with updates required only if major steps change. Simple high-level processes are easier to grasp and consume and they leave enough flexibility for an intelligent person to make adjustments as needed.

In his excellent book, *Systemology*,[46] David Jenyns advises that you create two-person teams to document systems: one person demonstrating the process and another one observing and documenting it. This allows the person documenting the playbook a level of objectivity and ensures that the process is understandable to an outsider.

The person executing the process may be doing it intuitively without realizing the precise steps they are doing that make the process work. A star salesperson may just follow their instincts in closing the sale, while an outside observer can detect questioning techniques, body language, and demeanor.

Removing the burden of documentation from the practitioner also motivates the expert employee to prioritize documenting it. All they have to do is perform their job and let someone else observe it.

Ideally, for each Playbook select a champion and a deputy champion to ensure you are covered at all times and there will be someone around to support the users of each playbook in the company. Coordinate vacation schedules to avoid overlap between the champions and their deputies.

Step 4: Obtain Feedback and Signoffs

Share the draft playbook with team members who participate in the process to ensure you have documented it correctly. Have an independent person review the documentation to ensure the playbook is understandable to a novice or a layperson. Have your process owner and responsible leader sign off on the document.

Step 5: Activate Your Playbook

Activate your approved playbook in your systems management software (see below), and inform the people who use the process that the playbook is now ready to be used.

Tips for Designing Playbooks

Start by Defining the Goal

To accomplish the Define Practice of the Playbooks Principle, begin with the end in mind. Define the result you want to see achieved for each playbook and work backward, as shown in Figure 7.3.

Figure 7.3: Process Goals Examples

PLAYBOOK	GOAL
Marketing Playbook	Generate leads for the Sales Function to be turned into recurring revenue clients.
Sales Playbook	Sell new monthly recurring revenue.
Project Playbook	Complete projects on time and on budget, without scope creep.
Accounting Playbook	Create timely and accurate financial statements, management information and tax returns.
Client Onboarding Playbook	Set client expectations, establish accountability and lay the foundation for a positive client relationship.

Describe the Steps Simply

Give each step a short title. The bullet points for each step include details of what the step is about. Here are a couple of examples:

Outside Sales Playbook steps:

1. The Goal
2. Lead
3. Follow-Up Call
4. Discovery Meeting
5. Prepare Presentation
6. "Findings" Meeting
7. Sign Agreement
8. Schedule Handoff Call

Client Onboarding Playbook steps:

1. The Goal
2. Handoff Call
3. Finance
4. Account Management
5. Operations
6. Setup Tools
7. Pre-onboarding Questionnaire
8. First-Week Activities
9. 30-Day Review

Draft the bullets for each step by describing the action in general without going into procedural details. See Figure 7.4 for an example. Assume the owner of the playbook is an intelligent person who will be able to implement the step.

Figure 7.4: Accounting Playbook example

GOALS
- To ensure we have operational cash!
- To ensure accurate accounts receivable and acounts payable
- To ensure timely accounts receivables and account payables

ACCOUNTS RECEIVABLE (AR)
- Responsible for billing process (see Billing Playbook)
- 80% of project hardware/software must be paid in advance by clients if order over $2,000
- Project labor will be billed as soon as the project is complete or a billable milestone is reached
- MSP tickets billed monthly (must be mailed by 5th of each month), Break-Fix weekly
- Must have tax-exempt certificate on each file for each tax-exempt client
- Manage "Collections" process (see Billing Playbook)

ACCOUNTS PAYABLE (AP)
- Review and pay bills twice/month (on the 15th and 25th)
- Pay bills on time (not early or late)
- Follow "Profit First" philosophy and pay accounts (on the 15th and 25th)
- Calculate and pay sales tax

EXPENSE REPORTS
- Review and approve expense reports each month
- Reimburse staff for approved expenses

CLIENT AGREEMENT/CONTRACT ANALYSIS
- Create all new clients contracts (e.g., MSP, Hosted Exchange)
- Review expiring contracts on the 1st of the month
- Discuss expiring contracts with vCIO before expiration (vCIO gets updated agreement)
- Extend/renew contracts when applicable
- Update existing contracts when notified by Central Services (e.g., Hosted Exchange mailbox added)

VENDOR CONTRACTS
- Review our vendor contracts/policies at least annually for accuracy and best pricing
  - Insurance (health, workers comp, building, contents, etc...)
  - Cell phones
  - Data and landlines
  - Other miscellanous contracts
- Track and pay for vehicle tags
- Renew insurances

PROFESSIONAL RELATIONSHIPS
- Manage and maintain relationship with bankers, accountants and attorneys
- Maintain credit score rating/info with Dun & Bradstreet

REPORTING
- Report usage stats to vendors when necessary. Report info should be gathered from "SaaS" and "HaaS" spreadsheets updated by Central Services person.
- Run monthly MSP profitability report and update budget
- Update as needed

Managing Your Playbooks

Appoint a person who will oversee the creation and storage of your Playbooks. David Jenyns advises that it is best to pick a systems management software (SMS) product to record your systems in. An SMS is a custom-designed solution in which you can create, store, assign, and optimize your systems.

Most people keep their systems in computer folders or a cloud repository such as Dropbox or Google Drive. Jenyns advises against this because a traditional file structure can lead to confusion, lack of clarity, and the loss of systems content over time. Systems that contain different file types, such as PDFs, videos, and Word files will have to be stored separately in subfolders, preventing the user from having a complete and coherent overview of the system.

An SMS, like SystemHub, which was developed by David Jenyns's company, offers some of the following features that help keep your systems organized:

- Videos and checklists embedded in each system documentation that can be viewed under the relevant step.

- Systems can be tagged and searched for easy access.

- The administrator can create permission levels so that each user sees the systems that pertain to them. No one can download the complete system library without your permission.

- Users can be digitally asked to approve and sign off on systems, so use and access can be centrally controlled.

- You can create custom learning tracks for new employees and observe how they progress with training on their systems.

- Templates and processes for creating new Playbooks and embedded videos are included.

Ideally, you want to Define and document your own Playbooks, but some companies never get there. If you would like help with that, check out Process Optimizer at processoptimizer.biz, which is specialized in documenting Playbooks for companies powered by Pinnacle.

Key Ideas from Practice 7: Define

- Your company will grow only to the extent that your leaders continually expand their impact by focusing on higher-value activities.

- Delegation requires Playbooks to enable less-experienced and less-skilled employees to execute work processes.

- Identify the most impactful Playbooks in your business and follow a five-step sequence to define, record, document, review, and activate them. Your Customer Experience and Employee Experience Playbooks are a great place to start.

- Consider selecting a systems management software system to store and manage Playbooks.

PRACTICE 8: INGRAIN

"We are what we repeatedly do.
Excellence is not an act, but a habit."

—Aristotle

Now that you have defined your most critical Playbooks, it is time to make sure everyone is using them. Your objective is to go from a business relying on the skills and experience of individual employees to a systems-based business that is not dependent on any single person.

This process requires a culture change and will take some effort and time to accomplish.

Broadly, there are five phases involved in ingraining your playbook culture:

1. Find a person who can take charge of running your business on Playbooks.

2. Sell your team on the benefits of running the business on processes.

3. Establish a system for playbook owners to manage their processes.

4. Have a strategy for and deal with resistance to the change.

5. Gradually expand the number of Playbooks to cover every part of your business.

1. Finding Your Second in Command

We talked earlier about the two potential senior leadership positions in a company: the Visionary and the 2IC. Small companies almost always start out with one leader, typically the founder who is the CEO, or equivalent leader. But where there are two or more founders, the two roles of Visionary and 2IC may emerge from the start.

Visionary entrepreneurs are often driven by the emotion of excitement around ideas. Some of these ideas are brilliant and can lead to moneymaking opportunities; others are fleeting. Though they love ideas, many entrepreneurs get easily bored by process and repetition and find it hard to focus on running daily operations.

The 2IC personality is just the opposite. This person embraces structure and processes, and they love to generate consistent results by organizing, empowering, and managing people and removing obstacles from their team's way. They love efficiency, repeatability, and high performance.

Ideally, you want to find a 2IC to put in charge of playbook management. This person may already be in your business waiting to be discovered. They may not be on the leadership team yet, and they may be young. Keep your eyes open and get that person involved. You want somebody who is confident and is not a pleaser so that they can drive accountability.

If you already have a 2IC, empower them to make decisions and manage the Playbooks without your involvement. You can always have regular check-ins to ensure you are on the same page and they understand your objectives.

If you don't have a candidate for the 2IC spot, try to identify a bright, ambitious, process-oriented person who communicates well. Make them responsible for organizing and coordinating your Playbooks.

2. Sell Your Team on Playbooks

It's human nature to resist change, and you want to get off to a good start. You want people to see systemizing your business as a positive change that will help them and the company succeed. Make sure you are enthusiastic about the shift and project the right energy in favor of the change.

David Jenyns lists the benefits for team members and the company of operating on Playbooks, which can be summarized as follows:

- Using Playbooks reduces errors and wasted time, and employees feel empowered because their managers can be more hands-off.

- It is less stressful for employees to go on vacation because other employees can run their processes while they are away and work does not pile up.

- Equally, it is much easier to onboard new employees, who can hit the ground running using their Playbooks.

- By documenting systems, people free themselves from repetitive tasks and can progress in their career to the next challenge, where they can make a bigger impact.

- Having documented Playbooks allows you to discover gaps in competencies and capabilities in the team, which can guide hiring decisions.

- The business benefits from leveraging best practices, which accelerates execution and improves consistency and quality.

- A systemized business is easier to run and can even become self-managing, allowing the owner to hand over management to a 2IC or even sell the business.

The best way to make your case is to listen to your employees and customize your arguments to address their specific concerns. Are they burning out? Is their learning curve flattening and they need a new challenge? Do they have potential to move up in your organization? Are they concerned about making mistakes or having to make too many decisions?

3. Establish a System to Manage Playbooks

Create a Playbook Ownership Chart (Figure 8.1) and assign each playbook an owner who is responsible for ingraining the process across your business. Set metrics to measure the effectiveness of execution.

Figure 8.1 Playbook Ownership Chart

NAME OF PLAYBOOK	PERSON ACCOUNTABLE	KPIs (BETTER, FASTER, CHEAPER)
BILLING AND COLLECTING PAYMENTS	Julie	100% invoices out within 5 days 90% of A/R under 30 days
RECRUITMENT	Julie	Open position filled less than 60 days All new hires are 8/10 or higher
CUSTOMER SATISFACTION/DELIGHT	Samantha	Average rating over 85% on surveys More than 20 "fix" calls per week
LEAD GENERATION	Paula	400+ qualified leads per week Lead acquisition cost less than $ 135
SALES	Istvan	4 warm leads per week 2 presentations per week
OPERATIONS	Samantha	Billable utilization more than 85% More than 90% of projects on time, on budget

Source: Adapted from Verne Harnish, *Scaling Up* (ForbesBooks, 2014).

Ingraining Playbooks includes three activities that the process owner must perform regularly. Booking time quarterly to execute these activities is good practice.

Step One: Train participants. Map out the people who will be involved in the playbook. For example, the customer experience playbook likely involves the salesperson and the sales manager. It may also involve an operations person who handles the onboarding of clients and an account manager who is responsible for "farming" the customer, offering them other helpful services.

Training may involve explaining the playbook followed by a process walkthrough, where an employee demonstrates the best practice of executing the process. Trainees then may roleplay with their trainer and ask questions.

Trainees leave with a copy of the playbook in hand and a commitment to practice the process in the coming week.

If you are storing your Playbooks in a systems management software (SMS), such as SystemsHub or Tallyfy, assign process training to employees who are going to use the playbook. You can monitor their progress as they complete their training.

Train your people to look to Playbooks as their first port of call whenever they have questions or don't know how to complete a task. Most employees will appreciate the independent access to company best practices Playbooks provide them, but adjusting may take some time for others.

Step Two: Track execution. What gets measured, gets done. If you want to ensure that the playbook is executed consistently, design metrics that gauge the frequency and quality of execution.

A well-known fast-food chain measures the frequency of its restroom cleaning process by having the responsible employee sign a rubric for each hour of the day when the restroom is cleaned. As part of the restaurant management process, the manager sporadically checks the bathroom for the integrity of the cleaner's recording and to log a 1 to 5 cleaning quality score.

The scores are entered in a scoreboard that is reviewed by the restaurant team in their weekly tactical meeting. The cleaning person meets the metrics if at least 90 percent of the rubrics are signed and the cleanliness score is no less than 4.5.

The advantage of using an SMS is that you can ensure Playbooks are followed. Require team members to tick off items in the system as they execute, confirming that they acted consistently with your best practices. Many of these applications have user-friendly smart phone or tablet versions as well.

Step Three: Coach your players. Below-standard metrics scores automatically are entered onto the list of topics for the Tactical Meeting, which participants prioritize and discuss after the accountability portion of the session. The reasons for a below-standard score may be that the responsible employee was overwhelmed by other responsibilities, they neglected their duties, or the playbook was poorly designed or is impractical.

After your Playbooks have been put together and you face a service failure, it can only be the result of one of two causes: either the scenario was not in the playbook, or the person wasn't trained properly.

For example, if the service personnel is running late, they are supposed to call the client. If they did not do that, then it is time to check the playbook. If this step is missing, it is not the employee's fault, and the playbook must be fixed. If the step is in the playbook, we have a training issue on our hands.

If the playbook needs to be improved or reviewed, the scribe of the meeting passes discussion notes to the process owner to investigate and improve the playbook or to retrain or coach the respective employee, as required.

The owner of the playbook is responsible for keeping track of all metrics and notes evidencing below-standard execution. Occasionally, participants need to be retrained or reminded of how to execute the playbook or where they can refresh their skills.

Playbook owners should consult the list of newly hired employees and their positions to consider whether any new joiners should be trained on their Playbook. This is also the time to review the performance of process metrics and simplify them where possible or necessary.

Figure 8.2 The Playbook Perpetuator

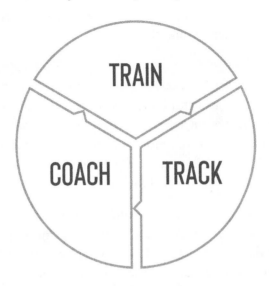

Groove Commerce, an e-commerce agency, defined its Playbooks in waves over the past five years. They started out selecting and creating 12 high-level Playbooks, each of which was owned by someone on their four-person leadership team.

These served them well until the business established a midlevel management team. This team had to create their own Playbooks so they could delegate to the next level of junior employees.

After continually growing the team, Groovers have recently started defining their third generation of Playbooks.

You can use purpose designed software to track your Playbooks such as the Pinnacle App[47] SystemHub, or Rubicon Software for Pinnacle.

4. Be Ready to Handle Resistance

It's your job to sell your team on using Playbooks, but that will not always be enough. *Systemology* mentions three types of resistance that you may encounter.

Job security. Some of your employees might resist documenting their work because they want to protect their power of being irreplaceable in the organization.

Many years ago, Steve witnessed how an IT director sabotaged the transition of a large commercial bank to new technology in order to protect his high-paying job. He was the only person who understood the system and recognized that a change would make him dispensable. It took 18 months of maneuvering for the CEO to dislodge him from his position. The bank lost millions of dollars and market share as a result of this delay.

Greg had a high-end architectural coatings manufacturer client where the plant leader refused to document paint recipes because "if he did, they could replace him." He thought it was a way to keep his job. Instead, his attitude led to his downfall, as it became obvious that the company could not scale with his type of thinking.

Hiding laziness. Documenting systems may pull the cover off of how little some team members actually do. You may have employees who are concerned that their job will no longer be justified post-systemization, and they might actively try to sabotage your playbook creation efforts.

Entitlement for long tenure. Long-timers sometimes develop a sense of entitlement that they feel they have earned through their years of service. Many may believe that Playbooks are for newcomers only and that they can carry on working intuitively outside the systems. Sometimes recent senior hires who grew up in a different culture don't want to relearn something "they know how to do best." These are tricky situations that require careful handling.

Years ago, Steve's business, MB Partners, hired one of his former peers who had run a subsidiary of the bank they both worked at. He was a great relationship builder with a pleasant personality, and he had deep domain experience. However, that person had a real problem with adapting to MB Partners' strategy, which was different from its competitors'.

MB Partners streamlined its business development process, which relied on a specific set of questions and language to convert leads into customers. This peer did not believe in this and preferred relying on his social skills to bring in business, but his approach was ineffective and discredited MB Partners' process in the eyes of junior employees.

He turned out to be an "old dog" that preferred to stay with his old tricks, and Steve had to painfully part ways with him. (Warning: Don't hire friends!)

5. Expand the number of Playbooks

To get your playbooks rolling, we suggested starting with the Employee Journey Playbook (Figure 7.2) and the Customer Journey Playbook (Figure 7.3). *Systemology* suggests picking the next 15 to 20 processes to document, as a second phase. These will be the most repeatable systems in your leadership level Functions, such as Operations, Finance, Engineering, Administration, etc.

From there, you can continue creating Playbooks in order of priority. We don't recommend eating the Playbooks elephant in one sitting, as you likely have bigger priorities in your company, at least in the early days of your Pinnacle journey.

Key Ideas from Practice 8: Ingrain

- Look for an in-house champion who is passionate about Playbooks.
- Enthusiastically sell your team on defining Playbooks.
- Follow a three-step approach to ingrain your Playbooks.
- Have a plan to neutralize resistance to the use of your Playbooks.

PRACTICE 9: OPTIMIZE

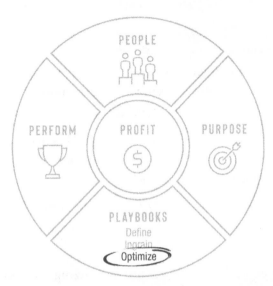

"You don't get any points in life for doing things the hard way."

—Tim Fargo

The magic of having your Playbooks defined and ingrained is that you can then start **optimizing** the machine of your business.

Playbooks can be optimized in two ways: by enriching or by simplifying them.

Figure 10.1: Two ways to optimize Playbooks

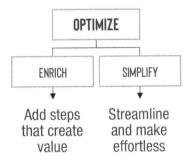

Enriching a playbook is to make it deliver more value. A client onboarding process would be enriched if you sent the new customer a "shock and awe package," thanking them with an impressive gift for joining your family of clients.

The other and bigger opportunity to improve Playbooks is to simplify them. It is critical to simplify, as complexity kills growth. There are almost infinite ways to simplify processes by removing redundant steps, eliminating bottlenecks, roadblocks, and by reducing waste.

An example of simplification is to use visuals instead of narratives. Describing how to load a truck can be a complex and confusing narrative. Instead, show a picture of what a truck looks like when it's loaded properly.

The ultimate simplification is to automate a process and eliminate any human effort in delivering it, while increasing customer value and satisfaction.

In this section we'll focus on optimizing Playbooks through simplification. This can be done in three phases, we call: analyze, eliminate, and automate.

The Three-Phase Simplification Formula

Figure 10.2 Playbook Simplification

ANALYZE	ELIMINATE	AUTOMATE
• Customer interactions • High value-add activities • Places when info is exchanged	• Bottleneck • Roadblocks • Waste (T.I.M. W.O.O.D.S.)	• Workflows • Touchless • Artifical Intelligence

Phase 1: Analyze

Scrutinize every step of the process to see whether it adds value or just adds waste including:

a. Customer interactions

b. High value-add activities

c. Places where information is exchanged

d. Bottlenecks, roadblocks, and other reasons for delay

In Practice: 7 Define, we told you the story of how Steve shortened documentation production at MB Partners from three months to three weeks. They did that by analyzing and modularizing the selling memorandum.

During that process, Steve and his team discovered that readers preferred the memorandum to be in a landscape format with a concise bullet point style and lots of pictures and graphics instead of the traditional narrative layout in portrait view.

They also noticed that a handful of sections were critical, while others were secondary, so they focused on the critical ones. It was also important to have an executive summary at the front and financials at the back.

Steve's team then broke up the memorandum. The financial parts involved lots of number crunching and chart formatting, which they delegated to junior analysts. The middle part required research and writing skills that took three to four years to master. These were done by managers. A vice president was in charge of putting the parts together, drafting a compelling narrative about the management group, and reviewing the work of the team.

There were eight sections in the memorandum, and production ran on parallel tracks by three-strong teams, but they could accelerate the process by adding more team members if they had people available. This helped them with utilization managing feast and famine periods in the flow of new projects.

Phase 2: Eliminate

Having analyzed your playbook for steps that fail to add value, slow or obstruct the flow or create waste, it is time to eliminate them.

Bottlenecks

A workflow bottleneck is a step that gets more inflows than can be processed. (See Figure 10.3.) That interrupts the flow and causes delays. Symptoms include repeated errors, increasing backlog, and unhappy customers and staff.

One of our clients, a water and fire mitigation company, developed a bottleneck in the estimating department every time there was freezing weather that broke water pipes and caused floods.

They would receive two dozen work requests daily, but they had only a single estimator on staff who could process no more than six to eight cases a day. It would therefore take several days to issue proposals for some customers, many of whom turned to other providers and were lost for this business.

Then, a couple of weeks after a weather event, the company would develop a bottleneck in the mitigation department because of a shortage of drying equipment. This frustrated customers because each day of delay exacerbated their flood damage and extended the period of discomfort they had to endure.

Our client's Yelp and Google ratings reflected its customers' unhappiness, eroding the company's market position.

Figure 10.3: Process bottleneck

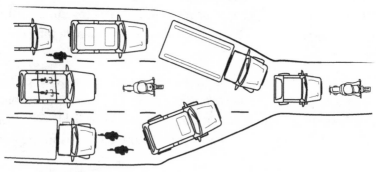

The challenge for our client was increasing the availability of estimators and drying equipment without building up excess capacities that could not be utilized in normal weather periods.

The profitable way to eliminate a bottleneck is to manage the flow and maintain even capacities slightly below the level of demand.

This mitigation company managed its flow by building a reconstruction department that employed multiple estimators in times of normal weather. When disaster struck, those estimators could be redeployed to prepare proposals for high-margin restoration projects.

The dryer equipment bottleneck was eliminated by securing rental equipment that could be shipped in from a network of other mitigation companies in geographies not impacted by the local weather event.

Roadblocks

Roadblocks may be caused by tactical issues or organizational impediments, such as a team member being pulled away for an ad hoc project, lack of equipment or supplies, or lack of access to a decision maker. Sometimes interpersonal conflicts between department leaders create roadblocks too.

Uncoordinated project dependencies can also cause roadblocks. Using a FAST Rock Planner (more on this in Practice 10: Rocks) helps avoids that by highlighting the importance of mutually agreed timetables and time-buffers to absorb ad hoc delays.

Email chains can also create roadblocks, when the ownership of responses gets murky. Solve this by keeping your Function Ownership Chart clearly defined. Replace email with centralized project communication applications, such as Slack.

Waste

Investigate your processes for signs of waste. A great framework to use is the Eight Wastes of Lean that employs the acronym TIM WOODS.[48] (See Figure 10.4.)

Figure 10.4: The Eight Wastes of Lean—TIM WOODS

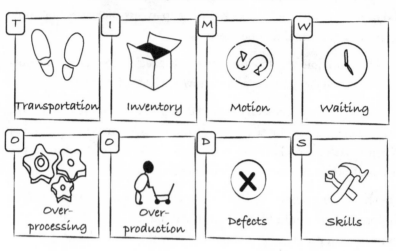

Source: Figure inspired by "8 Wastes of Lean TIMWOODS," Shmula.com, April 9, 2019, https://www.shmula.com/28695-2/28695/.

One of the biggest overlooked opportunities is avoiding the waste of unused human talent and ingenuity. This happens when you give your people insufficient training, place employees in positions below their skills and qualifications, and when you don't challenge staffers to come up with ideas to improve their work.

Phase 3: Automate

The ultimate optimization step is to eliminate human input altogether through automation. Here are a few simple steps to follow when considering automating your processes.

Starting with your current manual workflow, identify what needs to be automated. Is your goal to reduce the cycle time, improve throughput, or free people from menial tasks, like data entry, and move them to more productive activities?

Break down the processes selected for automation into detailed steps. There is no room to be high level here—machines *do* need to be micromanaged. The more detailed you get, the easier it is to automate.

Look for detail-oriented employees who love processes, numbers, and metrics. Perfectionists are welcome when it comes to automation.

Be ready to refine your workflow over time by establishing and tracking metrics.

Take time to research the right business automation solution for your specific processes. Look for tools that can handle multiple processes to cut your team's learning curve in implementation.

Workflow Automation

Reichle Klein Group (RKG), a commercial real estate and property management company in Ohio, picked the project management and workflow automation platform Tallyfy to automate their processes.

As Harlan Reichle, CEO, explains, "There are two stages to automating a process in Tallyfy. Stage one is to define the process. Stage two is to automate the workflow."

Defining the process is identical to what we described in Chapter 7. You map out the sequential steps and document these steps at a high level: who is doing what with what tool. A detail-oriented and intelligent employee can become proficient within a week in defining processes in Tallyfy.

Step two is automating the workflow. There are two levels of workflow automation. Level one is where the software tracks the accomplishment of your processes and triggers the tasks for participants to execute. (Level two is touchless automation that requires no human interaction. See more about this below.)

For example, when RKG lists a new property for sale, Tallyfy will prompt the listing agent to populate the information in the system to trigger a list of marketing actions.

When marketing has done their part, the facility managers will be notified that signs are ready to be displayed on the site.

Subsequently, advertising can be placed on Reichle Klein Group's website, third-party Web-listing platforms, and other media to promote the property.

The process owner can monitor execution using a dashboard, and all parties receive a daily email update for their outstanding tasks. Workflow automation can be programmed using a drag-and-drop low-code platform. If you would like expert help, Tallyfy will do this for you. Harlan told us that system experts charged about $40,000 for automating half a dozen key workflows at RKG.

OST Global Solutions, a 12 person consulting business, automated its processes using Mavenlink, a cloud-based automation solutions software specifically geared for professional services companies.

Co-founder David Huff described a similar experience with Mavenlink to that of Tallyfy. OST documented its processes, focusing on client delivery Playbooks, which prompted colleagues and contractors to execute different phases of client projects in a sequential and timely fashion. The process manager can track progress with a project dashboard.

A tech-savvy Pinnacle Business Guide, Ryan Giles, has automated over 70 processes in his practice using Zapier, and other automation platforms. This has allowed him to reduce administrative costs, the related risks of mistakes, and the burden of training and supervision. It has also increased the consistency and quality of service he delivers to his clients.

Touchless Business Processes

Recent years witnessed dramatic progress in full automation of processes using state-of-the-art Intelligent Automation technologies, also called "hyperautomation." According to Pascal Bornet, Chief Data Officer of Aera Technology, a company developing cognitive technology for the self-driving enterprise, Intelligent Automation (IA), is the "white-collar" version of "blue-collar" Industrial Automation that started in the nineteenth century.

Bornet explains that IA effectively creates a software-based digital workforce working hand in hand with the human workforce.

Its impact ranges from performing repetitive and low value-added tasks, to equipping workers with superhuman capabilities, such as analyzing millions of customer-datapoints and generating insights from them.

In his recent book, *Intelligent Automation*,[49] Bornet maps out the four clusters of technologies that empower intelligent automation systems:

1. **Computer Vision**: Optical Character Recognition and Intelligent Character Recognition allows the digitization of 80 percent of text and images for information and decision-making.

2. **Natural Language Processing** and Image and Video Analysis are used to interpret the digitized text and images.

3. **Data and Machine Learning** facilitates pattern recognition and allows software applications to predict outcomes without programming.[50]

4. **Smart Workflows and Robotics:** Workflow management tools use software robots to perform routine tasks. A software robot has a user ID just like a person and can perform rules-based tasks such as accessing email and systems, performing calculations, creating documents and reports, and checking files.[51]

Figure 10.5 The technologies driving Intelligent Automation

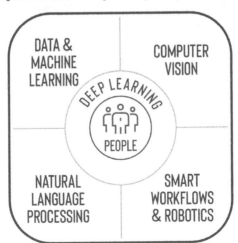

Source: Inspired by *Intelligent Automation* by Pascal Bornet.

Companies such as Aera Technologies design touchless workflows where some processes can be fully automated using software robots, called Robotic Process Automation (RPA).

The future of RPA is moving from rules-based automation to Artificial Intelligence (AI)– driven automation, where AI tools, including machine learning, will allow processes to optimize themselves over time.

Key Ideas from Practice 9: Optimize

- Your Playbooks can be optimized by enrichment or simplification.

- You can simplify by analyzing your processes and eliminating bottlenecks, roadblocks, and waste.

- The holy grail of systemization is automating your Playbooks and eliminating human interaction altogether.

Messages from Mountain Three: Playbook

Defining Playbooks allows you to delegate to people with less experience and less-refined intuition.

Ingraining your processes creates consistency and facilitates continual improvement. Over time, elevate your team by simplifying and eventually automating your Playbooks.

Systematizing the business allowed MB Partners to go from micromanagement to pods, and defining Playbooks liberated Steve as its CEO from project-execution and later from owning the sales, marketing, and management functions as well.

In the next chapter, we will show you how to create structured accountability and build the mechanism to engage your leadership team and the whole company in propelling your organization through vision-aligned and disciplined execution toward reaching your Purpose.

MOUNTAIN FOUR: PERFORM

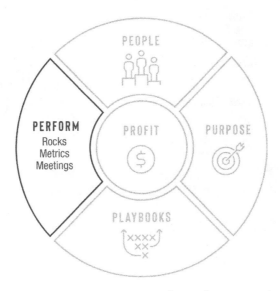

*"When performance is measured, performance improves.
When performance is measured and reported,
the rate of improvement accelerates."*

—Thomas S. Monson

Reliable Technology Services (RTS) is an MSP based in Baltimore, founded by two hardworking technologists, Lenny and Michael. Their intention behind starting RTS was to help small and mid-size businesses propel forward by using technologies. RTS grew rapidly by giving sound advice and putting clients first.

But the growth came at the cost of stress and long hours, and it stalled out when the four key employees in the business reached work capacity.

Lenny and Michael were already putting in 60 plus hours a week, and they needed to start working smarter.

So, how do you grow a business without burning out your best people?

Our business coach colleague from Denver, Richard Palmer-Smith, describes a company as a three-legged stool.[52] The three legs are: 1) your vision, 2) your strategy, and 3) structured accountability. With any of the legs missing or weak, you do not have a scalable business.

We have already discussed vision and strategy in the previous chapter, but what is structured accountability? Richard makes the case that it is about knowing "who is doing what," "who is reporting to whom," "what good looks like," and what your mutual expectations are.

In other words, structured accountability is a system of setting and achieving goals. Your vision cannot be achieved without systemizing your performance with the help of Rocks, Metrics, and Meetings. The next three chapters show you how to do that and climb Mountain Four: Perform.

PRACTICE 10: ROCKS

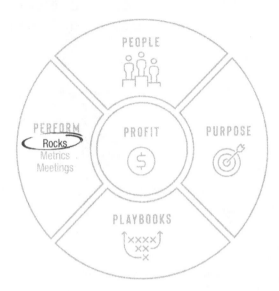

"If the big rocks don't go in first, they aren't going to fit in later."

—Stephen R. Covey

The best practice of goal setting evolved dramatically in the last 70 years from Peter Drucker's Management by Objectives (MBO) to John Doerr's OKRs.[53] The state-of-the-art approach is the practice of setting FAST Rocks. Rocks help you FOCUS, i.e., to Follow One Course Until Successful.

The term "Rocks" comes from Covey's famous demonstration of how urgent but unimportant tasks and distractions (pebbles and sand) squeeze out the less urgent but important Rocks, initiatives that move companies forward.

---

46 Austrian-born economist and father of the discipline of management, Peter Drucker started the movement by coining the concept of management by objectives (MBO). The essence of MBO is to engage people in setting regular goals aimed at fulfilling the company's mission in a cascading fashion.

One of Drucker's disciples was Andy Grove, back then, employee number three and later legendary CEO at Intel, who refined the concept into what he called objectives and key results (OKRs). OKRs build on the MBO foundation but make goals more tangible by defining the key results that need to be reached in a specific period, typically a calendar quarter.

The system of setting OKRs was popularized by John Doerr, an Intel alumnus-turned-eminent venture capitalist, in his book *Measure What Matters*. Verne Harnish, author of *Mastering the Rockefeller Habits* and *Scaling Up*, coined a similar term for quarterly OKRs; he calls them "Rocks." He borrowed the concept from Stephen Covey, who wrote *The 7 Habits of Highly Effective People* in 1989.

Covey proved that piling sand and pebbles into a glass cylinder fills up the space quickly, leaving no room for rocks. The solution is to put the rocks into the cylinder first, and let the pebbles and sand fall into the gaps between them so that everything fits into the glass. (See Figure 10.1.)

Figure 10.1: How entropy and focus companies work

Source: Figure inspired by Stephen Covey.

The implication is that successful companies commit to setting a limited number of **Rocks** each quarter that they can achieve over and above their day-to-day commitments. Then, executives hold each other accountable to making regular progress on these Rocks during the quarter.

For decades, the business community set "SMART" rocks, which were Specific, Measurable, Achievable, Realistic, and Timebound. This acronym has served us well, helping business leaders establish tangible goals.

However, in a 2018 whitepaper from MIT's Sloan School of Management,[54] Donald and Charles Sull made the case for a new acronym: FAST, which stands for Frequently Reviewed, Ambitious, Specific (no change there), and Transparent.

The new acronym aims to correct several failings of old school Rock-setting. Frequently reviewing quarterly objectives is a critical ingredient to accomplishing them. Too often Rocks got forgotten as soon as the leadership team left their quarterly offsite meeting, only to realize at the end of the quarter that their priorities have fallen by the wayside.

Figure 10.2: FAST Rocks

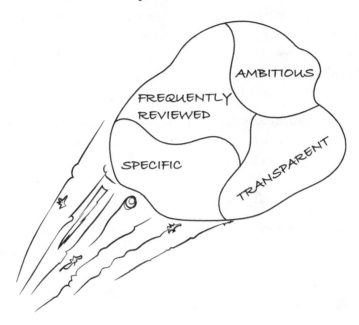

The SMART acronym's term "Achievable" often resulted in setting sandbagged Rocks. We prefer setting *Ambitious* Rocks that move the needle for the company.

Lastly, the secret of good Rock-setting is to make them Transparent and share them widely across the organization. Setting FAST Rocks is like quitting vaping: the more people in the company know about your resolution, the more likely you will be to accomplish it.

Strategic Planning

Beyond the MBO concept, Peter Drucker also taught us the concept of strategic planning. This is a goal-setting process that combines top-down and bottom-up approaches. (See Figure 10.4.)

It starts by reviewing the company's vision and strategy, making sure the leadership team is still inspired by the organization's Why and the long-term goal we call the Pinnacle.

Then come the Medium-term Milestones that we defined in the previous chapter. What will your organization look like at the end of the third (or if you want a longer medium-term plan, the fourth or fifth) fiscal year, say, December 31, 202X? You have set revenue and profit targets and established a metric that shows progress toward the Pinnacle (e.g., number of accountant hours saved, number of employees, etc.).

You have also broadly described the milestones that you must achieve by then (think structure, technology, markets, thought leadership, infrastructure, Playbooks, etc.).

Annual Growth Plan

Your Medium-term Milestones give direction for establishing a robust Annual Growth Plan. You start building the Annual Growth Plan by deciding your revenue, profit, and key metrics targets, as well as significant and tangible accomplishments that must be achieved on the way to accomplishing your Medium-term Milestones.

Most companies should start with determining their targetted "profit first,"[55] as there is no point growing revenues that don't contribute to the bottom line. (Unless you are a funded start-up in a race to grab market share.)

Let's say you decided to increase your net profit margin from five percent to seven percent this year. The obvious question is by what means will you achieve that goal? What actions will allow you to become more profitable? What will it take to charge higher prices for your offerings, and how will you constrain costs? The answer may be developing new products, entering new markets, or increasing efficiency by defining and optimizing your Playbooks. (More on that in Practice 14: Engineer.)

One of our Pinnacle Business Guides, Tip Quilter, created a tool called The Brutal Facts, which helps ferret out and validate your business's top priorities for the coming year. The tool is based on the story of Vietnam prisoner of war Admiral James Stockdale who had survived and helped many of his fellow prisoners survive years of captivity in North Vietnam.[56] His story was relayed by Jim Collins in *Good to Great,* pointing out that great leaders must never confuse the faith that they would prevail in the end while confronting the most brutal facts facing their business.

Another technique is to break down your Medium-term Milestones. What do you need to accomplish this year to move closer to your three- to five-year objectives? Your Pinnacle Business Guide will select the right tool to help figure out the correct goals for your Annual Growth Plan.

Ask your team to write each of their ideas on a yellow sticky note and post them on the whiteboard. Then move these ideas around into logical clusters, such as "sales growth," "people development," "product improvement," "documenting Playbooks." Assign each group of initiatives a pithy name that communicates to the whole company what your next year will be about.

Here are a few examples of annual goals from archetypal private businesses:

1. MSP

    a. Power the Engine
    b. Free Our Captain
    c. Build an Ark
    d. Let It Rain

2. E-commerce consulting firm

    a. Drive Impact
    b. Empower Our People
    c. Evolve Our Org
    d. Build Scalable Products
    e. Elevate Our Brand

3. Software company

    a. Level-Up Effectiveness
    b. Expand Product Portfolio
    c. Turn Ourselves into an Enterprise
    d. Turbocharge Sales

4. Distributor

   a. Rev Up Our Marketing Engine

   b. Zero In on Growth

   c. Level-Up Customer Service

   d. Demonstrate Our Expertise

   e. Upgrade Our Infrastructure

5. Fuel tax software for gas stations

   a. 12 Second Pit Crew

   b. NOS (nitrous oxide)—Start Your Engines

   c. Full Throttle On-boarding

   d. Right Car—Right Track

6. Heating and cooling residential company

   a. People FIRST!

   b. SOCKS: Simply Over Come Kinks in Service

   c. Tech UP!

   d. Drive ONE Trip

   e. Genz Connect

The more imaginative and relatable your goals are, the easier they will be to share with your company. Fun goals generate infinitely more engagement, and a higher proportion of them get accomplished.

FAST Rocks

Your annual initiatives or goals can be broken down into quarterly chunks called Rocks. Setting Rocks starts with the leadership team and cascades down to departments and sections of the company.

Most Rocks are driven by the annual goals you already set, as we described above. Occasionally, an important initiative arises during the year that takes precedence over the annual goals, such as an acquisition, replacement of a key executive, or responding to a crisis, but this should be an exception.

A good rule of thumb is to limit the number of Rocks to eight or fewer. No leadership team member should take on more than two to three Rocks, but one or two per leader is preferable. It is okay for a Visionary not to commit to taking on Rocks and to instead focus on supporting the team with accomplishing theirs.

It is good practice to have Rock owners create a project plan for accomplishing their priorities. This is the FAST Rock Planner we spoke about earlier, and it guides the owner of the Rock to define what is at stake with that Rock, establish internal milestones to achieving the final deliverables, and think through what may go wrong and how to mitigate such risks. (Again, the FAST acronym reminds Rock owners to *frequently* review these Rocks and make them *ambitious, specific,* and *transparent.*)

Figure 10.3: FAST Rock Planner

F.A.S.T. ROCK PLANNER

ROCK OWNER: DUE DATE:

ROCK TITLE:

DESCRIBE THE ROCK AND IS IT FAST?

Why is this ROCK important?

ROCK STEPS

BY DATE	ACTIVITY FOR ACHIEVING THE ROCK
First Step [+]	
Mid Step [+]	
Mid Step [+]	
Mid Step [+]	
Final Step [+]	

LIST RESOURCES NEEDED FOR COMPLETION

Setting Powerful Rocks

Rock setting is more art than science. We have facilitated over two thousand Rock-setting sessions between us, but still find small ways to improve the process. Here are a few principles to keep in mind.

Create Context

Help people understand how they should look at their business to uncover improvement opportunities. Tell stories of your own business challenges and of other companies' mistakes and solutions. Take pressure off people so that they don't feel inferior for not having experienced a seemingly obvious situation or for having made a "silly mistake." Don't judge people.

Ask Stupid Questions

So-called stupid questions are often the most productive because no one else dares ask them. It takes self-confidence and humility for someone to admit they don't know something or are confused. Often the confusion turns out to be warranted. Playing ignorant allows you to expose illogical arguments and inconsistencies that reveal where an urgent fix might be needed.

Give Clear Instructions

Be sure to define the task very clearly, say it in multiple ways, and get the team to feed back to you what they heard. People get distracted, and amazingly, C-level executives can still misunderstand a task that they had done 15 times already over the years.

Listen and Rephrase

Many private business executives are not adept at expressing their thoughts clearly. This can result in mistargeted or ambiguous Rocks. Listen intuitively for what team members are trying to say and simplify their sentences.

Always Ask for an Action Verb

The most critical word in any goal or Rock is the action verb at the beginning of the sentence. Without a clear action verb, there is no accountability and the Rock will be weak and vague. For example, compare the ambiguous "Customer Success Program" with "Launch Customer Success Program." Always ask for the action verb and help find powerful ones for your team members.

Ask How We Know It's Complete

The deliverable must be clearly defined so that everyone knows exactly whether the Rock has been completed. This is where "key results" from Andy Grove's OKR system come in. Make the outcomes measurable, if possible.

Using a Pinnacle Business Guide will shorten your learning curve to setting high-quality Rocks.

Aspirational vs. Committed Rocks

John Doerr talks about two types of OKRs: aspirational OKRs and committed OKRs. The same system can be applied to Rocks.

Aspirational Rocks are where you are swinging for the fences with a big or complex initiative. You can't realistically plan to complete it in the upcoming quarter, but you want to make substantial progress. You shoot for the stars, but landing on the moon is already a success. This type of Rock needs to be evaluated by your peers, and 60–70 percent completion deserves a green success rating, and 40–60 percent is a pass (yellow).

An example of an aspirational Rock is "onboarding 10 new distribution partners next quarter." If you get seven, this would be a successful effort, but you are stretching to get to 10.

The other type of Rock is the committed Rock. It is an all-or-nothing proposition. Either it's 100 percent completed or it's not done. Either you launch a marketing campaign or you don't. Either you get a new deal under contract or you don't. *Almost* closing a sale does not count.

Aspirational Rocks are most appropriate for fast-growing businesses that face a lot of uncertainty. Their advantage is that they force people to go from incremental ideas to completely reinventing their business. They are appropriate for highly ambitious and resilient people who are not crushed by sky-high expectations.

Most small businesses that provide services or distribute products benefit more from setting committed set-it-to-hit-it Rocks. These are black-and-white, and you won't need a committee of peers to evaluate them. In a context of reduced uncertainty, when you can rely on the achievement of committed Rocks, they offer less room for excuses and holding people accountable becomes much easier.

Figure 10.4: The Pinnacle Pyramid Phase 3: Annual and Quarterly Strategic Planning

Reasons for Missed Rocks

Learning to set great Rocks and to hit them is a discipline that builds over time. Nevertheless, here are the five pitfalls that cause 99 percent of missed Rocks:

1. **Not starting right away.** Rocks take time and often ninety days to accomplish. You will have to squeeze out slivers of time day by day throughout the quarter to complete your rocks while fulfilling your ongoing responsibilities. It is too easy to delude yourself into believing you would be able to catch up after a slow start. As Jim Rohn said: "Some things you have to do every day. Eating seven apples on Saturday night instead of one a day just isn't going to get the job done."[57]

2. **Lack of contingency planning.** Use the FAST Rock Planner to identify dependencies on colleagues, key resources, and outside parties. Build time-buffers into the plan, and create early momentum in order to leave yourself room to handle the inevitable challenges and delays.

3. **Picking too many.** It is best to limit your leadership team to five to seven Rocks per quarter and to make these count. No individual should own more than two or three Rocks.

4. **Boulder-size Rocks.** Don't try to boil the ocean in ninety days. Define an end-state for your Rock that you can achieve. An annual goal will often take multiple quarters to accomplish, so break it up.

5. **Not reviewing regularly.** Review your Rocks in your weekly tactical meetings (more on these later). Each leadership team member is responsible for completing the Rocks, not just the designated owner. Have each other's back.

Key Ideas from Practice 10: Rocks

- Rocks are priority initiatives that help you move your business forward every calendar quarter toward your vision and plan.

- By focusing on Rocks, you reverse the urgent-first, reactive mentality driving most organizations.

- Setting Rocks is both a science and an art that you can master by using a FAST Rock Planner and by following the principles described in this chapter.

After discussing Rocks that move the business forward, let's talk about how to deliver the ongoing activities that your organization must accomplish to make its quarterly numbers.

PRACTICE 11: METRICS

"What gets measured, gets managed."

—Peter Drucker

Nearly a decade and a half ago, when the fall of the Wall Street investment bank Lehman Brothers triggered the global financial crisis, Steve's consulting firm, MB Partners (MBP), faced a bleak future.

MBP's core business was to prepare small companies for sale and to find investors for them. With the looming uncertainty of an ongoing banking crisis and an impending global recession, its market slowed to a standstill. Investors put projects on hold until the smoke would clear and existing and prospective clients slammed the brakes on going to market, turning their attention to protecting their businesses as best they could.

MBP, too, had to retreat into defensive mode. Steve realized that the next 12 months would be about survival, which would need his laser focus on a daily basis. He let go of his A-Potentials and kept only the A-Players he could rely on to stay motivated and highly productive in the coming months, notwithstanding a 10 percent pay cut and the cancelation of 2008 bonuses.

Steve's business was on a knife's edge, and there was no room for error. The success fees representing 70 percent of the firm's income dried up immediately, and consulting fees, making up the remaining 30 percent, were much harder to come by. MBP's clients were going into cash conservation mode, so collecting receivables was inevitably more difficult, further reducing cash flow.

The firm had zero financial reserves and no recurring revenues to count on. Thus, they had to generate, execute, and get paid for enough projects each month to meet payroll, rent, and other essential overhead expenses just to live to fight another day. Since annual overhead was close to a million dollars, Steve had three monthly financial targets to hit:

1. GET WORK: Win $80,000 worth of new consulting contracts

2. DO WORK: Bill $80,000 of consulting work

3. GET PAID: Collect $80,000 cash from clients

In order to hit each of these three targets, they created a weekly scoreboard with the following metrics:

Figure 11.1 Metrics for the major functional areas of MB Partners

GET WORK

Metrics	Goal/Week	Week 1	Week 2	Week 3	Week 4
# of prospecting calls made	16	14	18	20	15
# of direct mail sent	200	100	250	300	150
# of 1st meetings held	5	2	5	6	3
# of pitches presented	2	3	0	2	1
# of proposals issued	1	1	1	2	0

DO WORK

Metrics	Goal/Week	Week 1	Week 2	Week 3	Week 4
Staff utilization	90%	93%	95%	90%	95%
% of projects on schedule	90%	95%	100%	85%	92%

GET PAID

Metrics	Goal/Week	Week 1	Week 2	Week 3	Week 4
Value of bills issued	$20 000	$0	$10 000	$15 000	$55 000
Cash collected	$20 000	$40 000	$10 000	$0	$30 000

Each Monday, delivery team members committed to 40 focused hours' worth of project deliverables and were expected to work overtime to meet their commitments, if necessary. This meant 100 percent expected utilization minus four hours for the Monday morning planning and scheduling meetings.

Maintaining the discipline of their Scoreboard week in, week out for the next several months saved MB Partners. Sales managed to keep the pipeline full, Delivery maintained consistent billing, and Finance collected the cash. After the summer of 2009, investors started coming back, and deals began to revive, allowing Steve's team to relax the discipline.

Gamifying Financial Performance

In his 1991 book, *The Great Game of Business*, Jack Stack tells the story of how he saved Springfield ReManufacturing Corp. (SRC), an engineering division of National Harvester that it wanted to shutter. Stack convinced his employer to sell him the division for $100,000 cash in a highly leveraged buyout so that he could save the organization and several hundred jobs.

Stack soon concluded that SRC could only make its quarterly debt payments if he engaged his employees in a quest. He called it the Great Game of Business, and it involved teaching people about finance and translating the expected personal contribution of each employee, from sales executive to shop laborer, into actionable metrics.

It wasn't just numbers. Stack engaged his team in building a vision, a strategy, and an execution plan, and he ultimately turned SRC into an Employee Stock Ownership Plan (ESOP). He effectively gamified the saving of the company. Today SRC is a 400-million-dollar conglomerate with a diverse portfolio of businesses around the United States.

Why Measure Weekly?

The idea of using weekly metrics is regularly challenged by CFOs and accountants as impractical and "overkill." It is hard enough squaring the numbers each month, with many businesses invoicing once a month and vendor bills trickling in late and erratically. There is also general resistance against timesheets and regular recording of activities, often labeled as "bureaucracy."

We admit it that creating weekly measurements can be a heavy lift up front and takes ongoing effort to maintain. Moreover, measures can fluctuate widely, making results look less useful. It also takes time and several iterations to figure out what to measure and what targets to set. Overall, it may seem like a daunting undertaking.

But here's the thing: when you only measure your results monthly, you get a historic report instead of actionable financial controls. Your accountant may not deliver your March numbers before mid-April, by which time you could be six weeks behind target. You are driving your car by looking into the rearview mirror.

On the other hand, an "impractical" weekly scoreboard gives you almost real-time control of your business. Did you miss your sales target last week? Then raise your activity level and get back on track right away. A weekly scoreboard puts you in control of hitting your monthly and quarterly numbers.

Consider your car dashboard. You only need about five real-time numbers to control your car. Fuel gauge; RPM (how hard your engine is working); speed (just passed a speed trap, how fast was I going?); battery; and oil pressure.

Input vs. Output Metrics

A frequent complaint about scoreboards is that the most relevant numbers cannot be directly influenced. How can you force a customer to sign a contract or pay a bill this week?

You can't, so try choosing actionable metrics instead, ones that statistically create the results you are looking for. Reverse engineer the level of content creation and social media networking activities required to generate a sufficient volume of leads for your business. How many RFPs must you respond to in order to yield the required number and value of contracts? How many billable hours should your staff produce for you to be able to invoice and collect your cash flow targets?

How to Derive Your Metrics

Start with identifying two or three metrics for each leadership-level function. These include the Visionary (if you have one), the 2IC, and each of the Functions reporting to the 2IC.

Figure 11.2: Function Ownership Chart, expanded to the direct reports of the leadership team

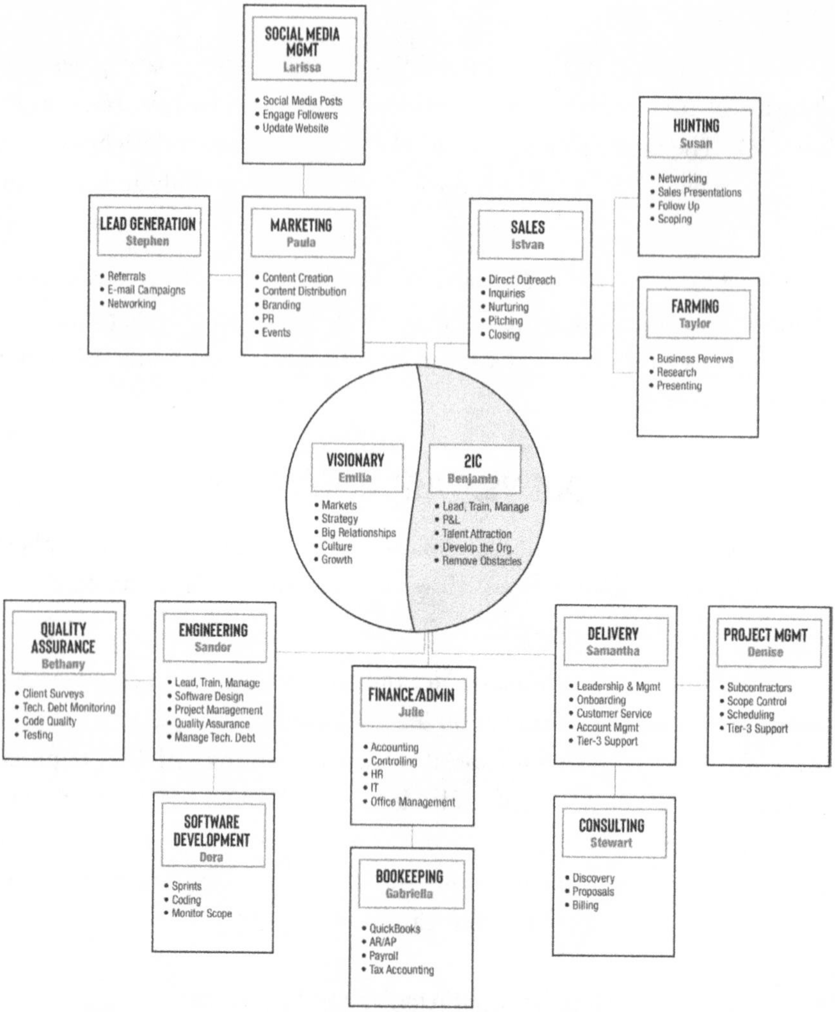

SOCIAL MEDIA MGMT
Larissa
- Social Media Posts
- Engage Followers
- Update Website

HUNTING
Susan
- Networking
- Sales Presentations
- Follow Up
- Scoping

LEAD GENERATION
Stephen
- Referrals
- E-mail Campaigns
- Networking

MARKETING
Paula
- Content Creation
- Content Distribution
- Branding
- PR
- Events

SALES
Istvan
- Direct Outreach
- Inquiries
- Nurturing
- Pitching
- Closing

FARMING
Taylor
- Business Reviews
- Research
- Presenting

VISIONARY
Emilia
- Markets
- Strategy
- Big Relationships
- Culture
- Growth

2IC
Benjamin
- Lead, Train, Manage
- P&L
- Talent Attraction
- Develop the Org.
- Remove Obstacles

QUALITY ASSURANCE
Bethany
- Client Surveys
- Tech. Debt Monitoring
- Code Quality
- Testing

ENGINEERING
Sandor
- Lead, Train, Manage
- Software Design
- Project Management
- Quality Assurance
- Manage Tech. Debt

FINANCE/ADMIN
Julie
- Accounting
- Controlling
- HR
- IT
- Office Management

DELIVERY
Samantha
- Leadership & Mgmt
- Onboarding
- Customer Service
- Account Mgmt
- Tier-3 Support

PROJECT MGMT
Denise
- Subcontractors
- Scope Control
- Scheduling
- Tier-3 Support

SOFTWARE DEVELOPMENT
Dora
- Sprints
- Coding
- Monitor Scope

BOOKEEPING
Gabriella
- QuickBooks
- AR/AP
- Payroll
- Tax Accounting

CONSULTING
Stewart
- Discovery
- Proposals
- Billing

To make this exercise easier, imagine it's Friday evening and you are driving home from the office after having had a great week. What outcomes made this week outstanding in the function you own? What two metrics did you hit to create the results for the outcomes defined in your Function Ownership Chart?

Pick the most important one or two outcomes and define a metric for each. Who is responsible for driving these metrics?

Keeping Score

You walk into a basketball game 10 minutes late, and you're wondering what you missed. You look up at the scoreboard and immediately know where the game is: There's 4:20 left in the first quarter and the Lakers are up 23–20 against the Warriors. LeBron James has the ball, and the shot clock shows three seconds of possession left. In the Score app, you can check the stats too in real time. Who are the lead scorers for each team, and how many passes, rebounds, blocks, and steals have they made?

You know who is currently winning, by how much, who is playing well, where the action is, and what to expect next. You have a clear picture of the game instantly, and you are having fun mentally weighing the statistics against records from other games, situations, and players. The scoreboard gives you, and every other fan and player, context, clarity, and anticipation.[58]

Without the scoreboard, players and the audience alike would be confused and disoriented. It would be impossible to play a suspenseful, fun game without one.

How about your company? Are you playing a suspenseful and fun game, or flying blind and hoping everyone would intuitively play well? How are you keeping score? How do you know your team is winning or losing?

Compile a Scoreboard

Eventually, you want to have full stats for the whole team, but for now let's begin with the starting lineup: your leadership team.

Having already defined the metrics for your executive team, use the following steps to create your Win-the-Week Scoreboard:

1. Create a spreadsheet with the following column headings from left to right: Function, Owner, Outcomes, Metrics, Weekly Target, and the Results for the week.

2. List your metrics on the horizontal lines, starting with the Visionary or the 2IC, and followed by your other function owners on your leadership team.

3. Establish weekly targets. A great way to do that is to take your annual planned number and divide it by 52, the number of weeks in the year.

4. Determine the number of metrics you need to hit to consider the week "won." You can ease into this process by setting a low bar (say, greater than 50 percent) and raise it over time as you iterate toward a helpful set of metrics with correct weekly targets.

Figure 11.3: Win-the-Week Scoreboard (see an enlarged version on page: 44)

FUNCTION	OWNER	OUTCOMES	METRICS	TARGET/WEEK	RESULTS	METER	WON?
VISIONARY	Emilia	# of followers Market share Market cap	# of big relationships touched # of talks, interviews, blogs	3 2	4 1		Y N
2IC	Benjamin	Profit Cash flow	# of coaching conversations # of talent prospect conversations	5 2	5 3		Y Y
MARKETING	Paula	Lead flow Social media engagement Brand awareness	# of qualified leads # of content pieces distributed	4 3	2 3		N Y
SALES	Istvan	Sales revenue New logos acquired	# of proposals issued $ of new MRR contracted	3 $5,000	2 $5,500		N Y
ENGINEERING	Sandor	Regular new releases Happy users	# of open tickets Staff utilization %	<=5 80%	2.5% 75%		Y N
DELIVERY	Samantha	Gross profit Growing existing customers	# of hours billed # of business reviews	600 2	625 0		Y N
FINANCE/ADMIN	Julie	Quickbooks is accurate & up to date Helpful and updated Scoreboards	$ of invoices issued Receivable days	$160,000 30	$180,000 42		Y Y
WON THE WEEK?							9/5

Keep these things in mind to establish a well-functioning scoreboard:

• Don't pick too many metrics—having five to fifteen metrics is ideal for a leadership scoreboard. If you have more, it will create too much noise, and you will not take any of the numbers seriously.

• Designate a clear owner for each metric. It's not who populates the number but the person driving it that counts.

• Focus on input metrics that its owner can action. "Number of conversations had, and value of proposals issued" is better than "number of contracts signed" even though the latter is the desired outcome of the former. We don't want pushiness to backfire nor to compromise contract terms just to make the weekly numbers.

- Appoint a scoreboard champion. Find someone passionate about creating, managing, and improving your scoreboard. Keep in mind that it would take months of iteration to produce a tool you are proud of.

- Roll out scoreboards to departments. As soon as the leadership team is comfortable with the concept, create departmental scoreboards. Pick one to three metrics for each subfunction on the Functional Ownership Chart.

- We recommend that you track the percent of your people who are A-Players or A-Potentials as well. This may be the single most important number for you to obsess over, as the right people in the right seats can solve any problem in your business.

Hitting your weekly Metrics will require executing your daily activities toward it. That completes your Pinnacle Pyramid. Your organization can fulfill your Why and achieve your Pinnacle, by reverse engineering the quarterly, weekly, and daily actions required by each member of your team.

Figure 11.4: Pinnacle Pyramid Phase 4: Tracking Performance with Metrics

Key Ideas from Practice 11: Metrics

- Break down quarterly financial goals into weekly, actionable metrics for each function and employee.

- Create scoreboards for your leadership team and departments.

- Gamify measurement by engaging all your people in winning the week and winning each quarter.

Now that you have Rocks and a Scoreboard, let's talk about how to use them. It's time to talk about Meetings.

PRACTICE 12: MEETINGS

"Most people spend more time and energy going around problems than in trying to solve them."

—Henry Ford

In the introduction to his business fable, *Death by Meeting*,[59] Patrick Lencioni shines the spotlight on a widespread problem: executives of private businesses often don't like meetings and consider them a necessary evil, even a distraction.

This is a shame, Lencioni points out, because meetings are a stage for the profession of leadership, in the same way that an operating room and the ice rink are the respective stages for the surgeon and the hockey player.

It might be better to accept that, as an entrepreneur or business leader, it is through meetings that you perform your most important function: leadership. Alone in your office, you may produce content and call and email people. But these are low-leverage activities compared to running great meetings where you can inspire, cajole, compel, and motivate multiple people, hold them accountable to get things done, and facilitate problem solving for your business.

Why Are Most Meetings Bad?

There are two reasons why most meetings are unpleasant and ineffective. First, they lack drama, and therefore they are boring. Second, they lack purpose and context. You can—and must—address both of these shortcomings.

The key is to identify and nurture the inherent conflict that exists below the surface. Why are you meeting? Something needs to be worked out, and there are probably plenty of obstacles to its accomplishment—that's the conflict. Bringing it to the surface helps create engagement, uncovers topics to explore and resolve, and repairs broken relationships between team members.

Hollywood directors and screenwriters know that without the drama of conflict, movies do not hold an audience's interest. The same is true for meetings. To make meetings interesting, participants must understand what is at stake and why it is worth investing their time in your meetings.

Therefore, you must start each weekly, monthly, and quarterly meeting by setting the stage and putting the right topics—often the most controversial ones—on the table.

However, no amount of drama will make up for a lack of context. Therefore, we will make the case for the different types of meetings and why they are essential for your organization and what is expected of their participants.

Meeting Structures

A high-performance business requires different types of meetings, each with a distinct function in communication and execution. Below is a list of the essential meetings that we encourage all our clients to embrace.

The Daily Standup

This is a daily five- to fifteen-minute check-in with your team to eliminate the noise of ad hoc communications among team members, to share important information, and to ensure clarity of action. It's literally a stand up, no sitting at tables, no video conference. Call in if you are remote. If you have nothing the team needs to know, you take a pass. You will find that if you are doing the daily standups correctly, they are a great time saver. They eliminate the "hey do you have a minute" chat or email and additional phone time. Your weekly tactical meetings will be less noisy, too, since you met several times last week to keep up with communication and ensuring your team was connected.

The three simple questions to ask your team members in a daily standup are:

1. What happened yesterday that the team needs to know?

2. What will happen today that the team needs to know?

3. Where are you stuck/where do you need help?

Figure 12.1: Meeting Structures

ANNUAL	**Planning**
QUARTERLY	**Strategic**
QUARTERLY	**All-hands**
MONTHLY	**Financial**
WEEKLY	**Tactical**
DAILY	**Standup**

The Weekly Tactical

This meeting is the stage for peer accountability in tracking the progress of Rocks, metrics, and one- or two-week action items and where the team identifies the list of topics impacting employees, customers, or business development activities.

This is where you identify, prioritize, and resolve critical problems and decide how to tackle challenges and opportunities.

You wrap up weekly tactical meetings by agreeing on who is doing what, what decisions have been made or information has been shared, and to whom your team should communicate.

We have realized over the years that topic lists often get overfilled by issues that should have been solved without the leadership team. Unwieldy topic lists overwhelm teams, who end up wasting time trying to prioritize instead of solving them.

To combat this problem, Greg developed a filter for meeting topics, which help whittle down the list to the important topics that the team needs to tackle. Ask the following question for each topic from the person who brought it, prior to putting it on The List for the weekly tactical:

1. **Is it something we really need to address?** Does it impact our Strategic Vision and Execution Plan or our Customer or Employee Journeys?

2. **Have you tried to solve it?** Surprisingly, executives bring topics to the table that they could solve themselves if they had taken the initiative. Leaders get paid for making decisions, so act your wage!

3. **Who can solve it, and have you talked to that person?** Most issues don't need the leadership team's deliberation and can be worked out in tandem with another leader on the team. Don't waste the group's time with these.

4. **What did you need to emerge from this conversation?** Do you need a decision, or do you just want to share information? Clarifying your objective will help you avoid tangents and tackle the topic faster.

Monthly Financial and Rock Accountability Meetings

This monthly meeting is a two- to four-hour meeting that replaces one of your weekly tactical meetings. You start by reviewing the prior month's performance against the budget, including your income statement, balance sheet, and cash flow statement (buckets).

Your leadership team needs to know the language of business, which is understanding the financial statements, what is in the various buckets, and how can you influence these numbers.

Leadership team members give updates on the progress of their Rocks, and you discuss how to get off-track Rocks back on track together.

Each leadership team member brings their FAST Rock Planner to the monthly Rock Meeting to show progress, ensure the milestones are on track, and get ideas and help if a Rock is hitting headwinds or fell in a crevice.

The leadership team owns *all* the Rocks, but one of the team members is assigned to drive each Rock, report on it, and sound the alarm when their Rock is in trouble.

This meeting also offers an opportunity to dive into one or two bigger topics that could not be addressed in the weekly tactical meetings.

Name Your Meetings

The Pinnacle approach is all about building a custom operating system for your company. Therefore, we encourage you to come up with your custom names for your meetings that reflect the character of your business. This is a part of Integrating your vision and strategy into your business. In particular, it is worth naming your Daily Standup and Weekly Tactical meetings.

Examples:

1. **Sealing connectors company**: Daily Quick Connect and Weekly Leak Test meetings

2. **Propane gas supply company**: Daily Pressure Release; Weekly Tank Tactical

3. **MedTech business (using saliva samples)**: Daily "Spit it Out" meeting

4. **Energy efficiency company**: Daily 917 Express (held at an odd time, to have everyone be punctual) and GSD Tactical (Getting Sh*t Done)

5. **Residential HVAC**: Daily "FITFO" (military term: Figure it the F*ck Out)

Peer Accountability

The secret of the Pinnacle Process is that execution is powered by peer accountability: team members report their progress in completing Rocks and achieving target metrics weekly, and they review financial and goal performance quarterly and annually.

Compared to traditionally managed private businesses, where the owner or CEO is the main source of accountability in an organization powered by Pinnacle, team members report to their own peers.

The fact that everyone could have an excuse makes excuses practically irrelevant. No one likes to look bad in front of their colleagues by not executing and letting the team suffer for it.

A-Players want to work with other A-Players and naturally marginalize or force out B- and C-Players over time. Your employees will do the heavy lifting holding each other accountable so that you don't have to.

Topics, Decisions, and Actions

Beyond creating peer accountability for progress (Rocks) and financial performance (metrics), weekly tactical meetings are designed to identify, prioritize, and tackle problems. Things that are getting in the way of your executing your Playbooks and delivering on your promises to your employees and customers should be addressed in your weekly tactical.

Small business leadership teams often get frustrated in meetings when meandering discussions fail to result in decisions and actions. People are good at talking, but often fail at listening, which is a harder discipline. To remind yourself of this, scribble WAIT on the top corner of your notes: "Why AM I Talking?"

Another failing is when a leader waits endlessly for a consensus to emerge or when they want 100 percent information before making a decision for action. This is a grave mistake. Not making a decision is called drifting, and it is the most dangerous (passively taken) choice.

In Pinnacle we like to solve decisions using the "Observe, Orient, Decide, and Act" (OODA) Loop process. This tool was originally developed by fighter pilot John Boyd for the US Military.[60] The OODA Loop is a practical concept that focuses on filtering available information, putting it in context, and quickly making the most appropriate decision.

1. **Observe**. What are you seeing? State the title of the issue as written on the weekly tactical topic list. Who owns the issue?

2. **Orient**. What is the crux of the matter? How would it read on a bumper sticker? Ask clarifying and probing questions to discover what is at the root of the issue. Restate it.

3. **Decide**. Canvass the group for solutions for the restated issue. Try to reach consensus on a solution. If no consensus emerges, let the leader of the meeting make a decision. Don't wait for perfect information, as you can miss the boat. Not making a decision *is* a decision that sometimes will hurt you more than a bad decision that can be corrected.

4. **Act**. Assign an Action Item to someone who agrees to carry out the decision. If the action required will take longer than one or two weeks to execute, put the decision on your Strategic Vision and Execution Plan topic list. Get the owner of the Action Item to affirm they will carry it out.

In some cultures, like in Japan and the Netherlands, no decisions are made until a consensus is reached. This is not workable in a private company that has limited capital and market power and therefore has to react to dangers and opportunities in real time.

A timely decision with 70 percent information available is better than a late decision made with 100 percent of the information. The benefit of a fast decision is that you immediately start receiving feedback about whether the decision was right or wrong and you can move to correct it. Refraining from making decisions gives you no valuable input to work with.

Productive discussions in meetings require your team to have confidence that everyone can freely speak their mind and there is no punishment for voicing a sensitive question or challenging assumptions.

In his bestselling book *The Five Dysfunctions of a Team*, Patrick Lencioni makes the case that the major dysfunctions of teams, including fear of conflict, lack of commitment, avoidance of accountability, and inattention to results, all stem from the fifth dysfunction: a trust deficit among team members.[61]

Consequently, by strengthening trust, you can mitigate all these dysfunctions. Trust can be built over time by asking team members to share personal information with each other in weekly and quarterly check-ins, and by facilitating the giving and receiving of constructive feedback with team-building exercises.

The Five Animals

A friend of ours and fellow business coach, Mike Kotsis, wrote a blog post about the four animal figurines that he brings to leadership meetings to help his clients communicate more openly.[62] They are an elephant, a cow, a bull, and a horse. We have added a fifth: a squirrel.

By formally introducing the animals and what they represent and requesting they be called on as needed, we give our client teams permission to raise difficult subjects. With the plastic animals present, anyone can grab one and broach a sensitive topic in a playful manner. (See Figure 12.2.)

Figure 12.2: The five animals that help keep conversations healthy

Elephant. The elephant in the room appears in most small companies from time to time. A person or behavior detrimental to the business is being tolerated by the owner or leader, and this is widely known but too sensitive a subject to talk about.

Perhaps the COO is too abrasive, or an employee who is a friend of the owner is not pulling their weight, or the owner's spouse has a no-show job.

The elephant, or its impact on morale, is often a blind spot for the owner, but it is toxic for the business. The elephant must be called out, discussed, and dealt with.

Bull. The bull represents two negative behaviors that need to be quashed: bullying and bullsh*tting. The former is the bigger problem, and it more often manifests as passive-aggressive behavior, but not always.

During a recent Pinnacle session, the 2IC of the business lashed out at the head of operations, attacking him in front of the group for his "subpar" performance. The rest of the team, including the Visionary, sat around passively, saying nothing. At the end of the 2IC's rant, Steve quietly pointed at the bull, which was standing in the middle of the table. The Second in Command angrily picked it up and threw it at him, upon which everyone, including the 2IC, broke out laughing.

Steve then turned to the Visionary and asked him if he wanted to say anything. Everyone was watching him and after 10 long seconds, he emphatically told them how frustrated he was watching that abrasive behavior and how it must stop. The 2IC sheepishly accepted the dressing down and promptly apologized to the head of operations.

The discussion that took place in a rented office got so heated that the receptionist walked in and asked the group to tone it down. However messy, this quarrel turned out to be a great relief for the group, all of whom, including the 2IC, rated the meeting a 10 out of 10.

Cow. Sacred cows must be slayed. The sacred cow is a pet project for a powerful leader in the business that is causing distraction and draining resources without a real upside. It perhaps had potential in the past, but it no longer makes sense, but no one dares to speak up and frustrate the project owner, who is in denial.

One of our clients, a consulting firm, had a sacred cow that was refusing to die. The company has been a system integrator for decades, struggling with productizing its services to make the transition to the cloud age. The owner came up with the idea that they could design a mobile retail unit to be operated as a business inside the business, which he thought might solve their scaling challenges.

The project was clearly outside of the company's core business, and they had no experience, expertise, or strategic relationships to support it. Soon it became a major distraction to the owner, impacting sales and delivery of core services. Thankfully, the plastic cow came to the rescue: the team redlined the project, and it was phased out soon after.

Another client focusing on multifamily property syndication struggled to give up two sacred cows that absorbed about 20 percent of the energy of the business. These included a coaching business inside the company, serving a different target market and producing negligible revenues at the cost of hundreds of hours of employee time, including from the two founders. The other sacred cow was an annual immersion conference organized for clients and prospects, that leadership was emotionally invested in, but which lost the company money.

After the guide questioned whether these were sacred cows, the team piled on, passionately making the case that the company should get out of these limited-upside loss-making ventures. The two owners eventually came around and ended up relieved and re-energized by the slayings. (Incidentally, both founders were Hindus, which may have greatly exacerbated the challenge. ☺)

Horse. In business, you'll occasionally witness a discussion where the parties just cannot reach consensus. Arguments become ever more repetitive and heated, without converging opinions. We call this "beating a dead horse." It is time to leave the dead horse alone, the leader must break the tie, and the team should move on to the next topic.

Dead horses are often caused by an indecisive leader who would rather wait weeks than make a decision that might alienate some members of the team. In reality, disagreeing team members are more frustrated by not getting a decision that would put them out of their misery. Few people expect their leaders to make perfect calls all the time. Just decide, move on, and course-correct later, if needed.

Squirrel. Finally, the squirrel serves as a reminder that the group has strayed into a tangential discussion. When driving, you sometimes witness a confused squirrel that cannot decide which way to run in front of your car. You see them doing the same on trees, jumping from one to the next and back again without any apparent focus.

Keep the discussion centered by noticing and calling out squirrels so that you can return to the topic at hand. If a squirrel emerges instead as a priority, put it on the topic list for later discussion. The roads of the world are paved with squirrels that couldn't decide.

Key Ideas from Practice 12: Meetings

- Meetings are the forum for team communications, peer accountability, and problem solving. Build an appropriate meeting structure that delivers on these tasks.

- Solve problems by following the OODA Loop (Observe, Orient, Decide, Act) for effective decision making.

- Leverage tools like the five animals to create a safe space for difficult conversations.

Messages from Mountain Four: Perform

The fourth Pinnacle Principle is Perform, which is achieved by mastering the Practices of Rocks, Metrics, and Meetings.

Your vision is executed through implementing structured accountability. Accountability is best achieved by leveraging peer pressure, and it takes place in meetings reviewing Rocks and metrics and by practicing disciplined problem solving.

For healthy, open discussions to take place, trust between team members must develop. This is stimulated with the use of check-ins and exercises for giving constructive feedback. Feel free to use props, such as the five animals, to break the ice and give people permission to bring up difficult subjects.

By mastering the three Pinnacle Practices of Perform: Rocks, Metrics, and Meetings, and by applying the peer accountability tools discussed in this chapter, Reliable Technology Services turned itself into a functional team and generated record growth and profit in the first year of their Pinnacle journey.

Having climbed the mountains of People, Purpose, Playbooks, and Perform, let's now discuss how to take Profitmaking to the next level.

MOUNTAIN FIVE: PROFIT

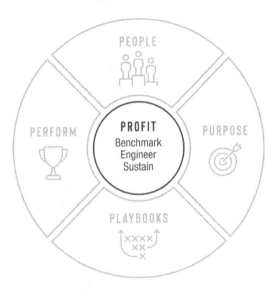

"A business without a path to profit isn't a business, it's a hobby."

—Jason Fried

Your profitability is an indication from the marketplace of how valuable your services or products are perceived to be. You can increase your profit margin by making your product and service more valuable at the price point you offer.

In the early 1970s, Japanese automakers Honda and Toyota flooded the American car market with inexpensive, fuel-efficient, and reliable cars at price points 20–30 percent below their U.S.-made rivals. The Japanese car brands were little known and little trusted at the time, and the manufacturers had to offer a substantial price advantage for the Honda Accord and the Datsun Violet to be competitive with the Ford Pinto and the Chevrolet Vega.

They did this by using a technique called value engineering. The Japanese car makers set a price point that would be competitive and then reverse-engineered a car and a manufacturing process that could deliver it profitably from that point.

Twenty-five years later, Hyundai and Kia applied the same approach. As newcomers, they had to offer substantial discounts to compete with Toyota, Honda, and Nissan, which by that time became highly regarded brands. The Korean challengers profitably offered reliable and well-equipped models about 15–20 percent below the Japanese automakers' prices.

Hyundai and Kia made enough profits to expand rapidly and promote their brands aggressively by sponsoring the Olympic Games, the World Cup, and other high-profile sporting events.

More recently, Elon Musk applied the same principles at SpaceX and Tesla. Space travel's greatest impediment has been the high cost of transport. It cost $54,500 for the Space Shuttle to propel a kilogram of payload into orbit, which the SpaceX Falcon 9 could do at 1/20th of that cost 10 years later.[63]

Tesla, another Elon Musk company, developed a similar advantage over its competitors when it comes to the fuel efficiency of its electric cars. The Tesla Model X LR's core efficiency is 25 percent better than its closest non-Tesla competitor, the Hyundai Ioniq.[64] Musk achieved these results by resolving to be substantially better than its rivals and engineering rockets and cars to deliver his targeted results.

In this chapter, we will examine how *you* can engineer your business to be price competitive while generating the profitability of the top-septile players in your market niche—in other words, how you can reach Pinnacle profitability.

You do this in three steps. The first step is to apply the Pareto principle and **Benchmark** your business against your peers to determine the net profit margin of the players that represent the top 16 percent in your industry segment.[65]

The second step is to consider how you may position yourself as a premium provider in your category. This is how you **Engineer** your cost structure and economies of scale so that you, too, can reach Pinnacle profitability.

In the final step, you build a stack of differentiating activities to defend your profit margin and **Sustain** it over the long term.

PRACTICE 13: BENCHMARK

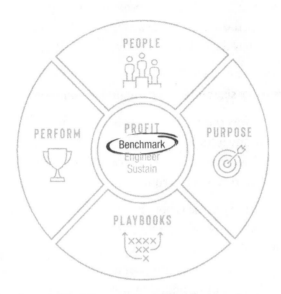

"Benchmark your performance against your best competitors. Think how you can beat them next time."

—Brian Tracy

After selling his business and moving to Virginia, Steve pondered what to do next. He knew almost nobody in central Virginia and had little knowledge of where to even begin building a network.

Years earlier, he had formed a mastermind group of business owners in Budapest, Hungary, and thought he could try to do the same in his new home town. He joined Vistage as a franchisee, and in the next 18 months launched two groups in Richmond, Virginia, one for small business owners and another for larger companies.

These groups met monthly to share experiences and operate as advisory boards to their members. They also regularly invited subject matter experts to deliver three-hour workshops on topics like sales, marketing, building teams, and financial management.

One of the speakers was a highly analytical person who talked about a fascinating, little-known resource. It was an annually published almanac that contained detailed financial information in aggregated form that the IRS extracted from the tax returns of a representative sample of over 110,000 of the approximately 5.8 million active corporations in America in 2013.

The almanac contained line-by-line tax returns of these companies grouped by revenue size and broken out into 94 minor industry segments.[66]

The almanac was out of date by then, but Steve tracked down a used copy on Amazon, and it turned out to have had an accompanying CD where the information was accessible electronically. For a former accountant and investment banker, this was the equivalent of a treasure trove.

Thankfully, this database is now available online for free from the IRS.[67] The only downside is that the published information is several years old. However, profitability trends at industry levels don't change that quickly, and you can benchmark yourself against your industry using these numbers. You can also normalize the information by averaging multiple years to remove the impact of the economic cycle.

Within a few weeks of receiving the book and CD, Steve had crunched the numbers and rearranged the information into a benchmarking tool that enabled him to compare his clients' key expenses and profit lines in their profit and loss statements with those of other companies in their industry segment.

For example, he isolated the top 16 percent and the bottom 16 percent of the list by revenue (one standard deviation from the mean in each direction) and computed the average performance for the Specialty Trade Contracting category. This is a broad group encompassing niche construction firms that specialize in such areas as roofing, carpentry, concrete work, heating and ventilation, and electrical contracting.

Figure 13.1: Benchmarking your performance to the top 16 percent of your industry

One of the first benchmarking exercises was performed for a siding contractor; let's call it Acme LLC. The owner had shared statistics about how his business was doing. Steve then compared the gross profit and net profit performance, respectively, to the bottom, the top, and the average performers in his industry group. He also analyzed the company's overhead to see how it was doing in major cost categories against its peers, such as payroll, advertising, and rent expenses.

As you can see from the following charts, there is a wide gap in performance between the bottom and the top 16 percent of industry players. You definitely want to figure out how to be in the latter group—the top septile. (We use top and bottom "septile" (1/7th) as a rough synonym for the top and bottom 16 percent, respectively.)

In Figure 13.2, there is a seven percent gap between the gross profit margins of a top-septile player and a low-septile one in a construction-related industry that operates at moderate margins. (Gross margin is gross profit divided by sales. Gross profit is the income earned by the company after paying for cost of goods sold [COGS], subcontractors, and any direct labor costs involved in delivering the work, and before paying for overhead expenses.)

Figure 13.2: Benchmarking Acme LLC's gross profit margin to the top-, average-, and lowest-septile performers in the Specialty Trade Contracting sector

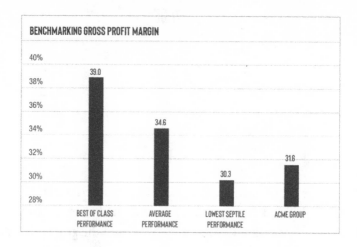

Benchmarking Acme's net profit margin (profit before tax as a percentage of sales) shows that Acme does slightly better than average, but almost nine percent worse than the top echelon. (See Figure 13.3.) This gives the company plenty of room for improvement by researching and emulating best practices, scaling, and so forth (of which more in Practice 14: Engineer).

Figure 13.3: Benchmarking the net profit margin of Acme LLC to the Specialty Trade Contracting sector

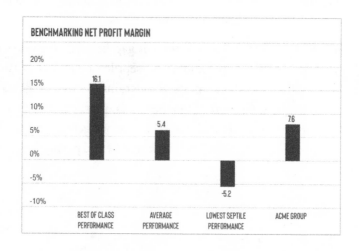

To find out more about where Acme is ahead and behind in its overhead, the IRS data allows you to benchmark certain expense items, such as payroll, advertising, and rental expenses, against those of peers. (See Figure 13.4.)

In this example, Acme LLC enjoys slightly lower payroll costs than its average brethren, but almost three percent higher costs than top contracting companies. This may be explained by regional differences in wages or the relatively small size of Acme compared to its top-of-the-class competitors, because profitable businesses have the means to grow faster than the rest of the field.

Acme ranks in the middle of the pack on advertising spend effectiveness (0.4 percent of sales) but head and shoulders above the field as measured by rental expenses over sales. The reason for this could be a combination of Acme's premises being located in a low-cost, semirural area and the company's reliance on subcontractors, which allows the core, employed group to make do with a small office. The company's warehouse is owned by the owner's other company, further reducing rent.

Figure 13.4: Benchmarking other expenses of Acme LLC to the Specialty Trade Contracting sector

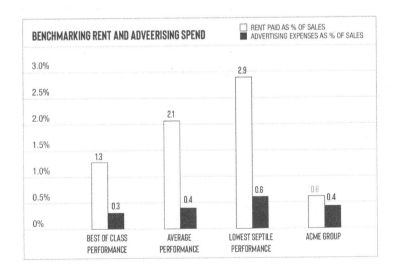

As the example demonstrates, benchmarking is just the first step in the analysis of what can be improved. Acme's main opportunity of improvement is controlling its COGS by cultivating its subcontractor base and possibly growing the business to have more leverage with material suppliers.

Scaling Acme will help reduce payroll cost percentage, as the leadership team, representing the heaviest payroll burden to the company, will manage more junior employees.

Profit First

Using the IRS's free database is not the only way to benchmark the financial performance of your business. Industry associations often collect confidential financial information from, and share it in aggregate form with, their participating members.

Self-organized industry mastermind groups also do the same. In the construction industry, there are "Twenty Groups" operating in noncompeting geographies. Each of these groups of about 20 peer companies get together regularly to share best practices, and often this includes sharing numbers.

A managed services provider (MSP) client of ours is part of such a group of other IT service firms, called MSP-Ignite (msp-ignite.com), that share information. In that same space, there are companies, such as Service Leadership (service-leadership.com), that provide regular benchmarking information and prioritized best practices advice to subscribers for a monthly fee.

Another resource for small companies is Mike Michalowicz's book *Profit First*. The premise is that you should "pay yourself first." The book argues that business owners should not squander their profits on superfluous expenses and mindless expansion only to have little or no bottom line at year's end. Instead, they should behave like responsible corporate employees who stack money away each month in 401(k) and other savings vehicles.

To determine how much money you should be saving, Michalowicz offers a commonsensical approach to determining the ideal profitability level of a small company. He introduces the concept of "Real Revenue" to calculate the required profitability for a small business, where more than 20 percent of revenue represents COGS or cost of sales (COS) types of pass-through expenses.

Real Revenue is calculated as your top-line revenue, less what you paid for materials and subcontractors to deliver your service or product. (See Figure 13.5.) This is similar to gross profit, but it excludes your direct expenses, such as employee labor costs and referral fees tied to delivering products and services.

Figure 13.5: *Profit First's* recommended profitability and owner's take

	A	B	C	D	E	F
REAL REVENUE RANGE	$0– $250K	$250– $500K	$500– $1M	$1M– $5M	$5M– $10M	$10M– $50M
REAL REVENUE	100%	100%	100%	100%	100%	100%
PROFIT	5%	10%	15%	10%	15%	20%
OWNER'S PAY	50%	35%	20%	10%	5%	0%
TAX	15%	15%	15%	15%	15%	15%
OPERATING EXPENSES	30%	40%	50%	65%	65%	65%

Source: Mike Michalowicz, *Profit First* (Penguin Random House, Westminster, MD, 2017).

Michalowicz argues, that, as the owner of your business, your profit, including your salary, should be at least 20 percent of your Real Revenue on sales of at least $1,000,000. We believe that targeting 20 percent profitability is a good general guide, unless you own significant intellectual property or have a highly scalable business around technological innovation or have access to a limited resource, in which case elite profitability will be higher.

In some commoditized industries, such as construction, 20 percent may be challenging to reach, and in our example above the top septile of the Specialty Trade Contractor sector generated over 16 percent net profit.

Generally speaking, businesses with less than double-digit margins are unattractive to investors because they are seen as commodities and they have little margin for error to withstand economic or industry shocks.

What Is Your No Man's Land?

The same IRS data enables you to benchmark your industry to ascertain those revenue sizes where profit margins temporarily dip. This happens when stair-step investments are needed to break through certain revenue ceilings, and it takes time to build the economies of scale to cover those investments.

Other reasons for stalled profit margins include the challenge of managing larger groups of people and the cost of creeping bureaucracy. In a bigger company, B-Players are less visible to even the most results-obsessed ownership group. Larger companies also manage expenses using budgets, which is a necessary evil, because spending becomes more mechanical, and defending budgets becomes a power-building tool.

The concept of the "No Man's Land" was coined by Doug Tatum, a management consultant and college professor, and is explained in his book of the same title.[68]

In Figure 13.6, you can see the overall landscape for all companies. Average net profit margin for the lowest category reviewed is over five percent, which starts to dip as sales revenue passes the $2.5 million mark, and it does not recover until the business passes $10 million in sales.

This is the No Man's Land for all small companies, and you have to get through to the other side to attract strategic or private equity investors. Companies in the No Man's Land tend to only attract owner-operators who will pay a much lower multiple because they will themselves be generating much of the value for the business.

After traversing the No Man's Land, your net margin steadily rises as your business scales up, builds market power, and hires trained executives.

The first No Man's Land chart in Figure 13.6 shows the pattern for construction companies. Small construction companies are often more profitable than larger ones because an owner-manager can make all the decisions and can directly control the team's performance.

However, as the business grows, it needs to build out a management layer, and the owner's control becomes indirect. It will take time and economies of scale to recover the cost of that management layer.

Another factor is that the productivity of salaried managers is often lower than that of the owner, who is fully financially exposed to both good and poor performance.

You can see in the first chart in Figure 13.6 that profitability recovers somewhat as the company crosses the first No Man's Land and enters the $10–$50 million revenue range.

For the construction group, there is a second No Man's Land that kicks in around $50 million in annual sales. The market here becomes more competitive, possibly as players have to step out of their home markets to grow. At that level, another management layer becomes necessary, further diluting the direct control of the ownership group.

At the $250 million mark, businesses again become more profitable because the number of competitors drops at that size level and acquisitions enable participants to harvest cost synergies.

Large companies also enjoy increased purchasing power and can negotiate discounts on material and equipment purchases. A robust balance sheet also supports bidding for large projects, where sponsors often demand extensive guarantees, which reduces competition.

Figure 13.6: The No Man's Land

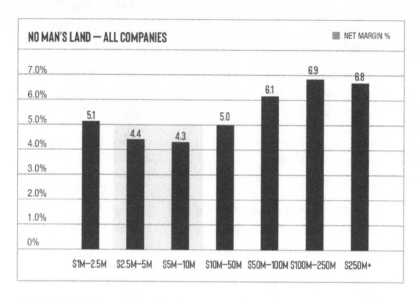

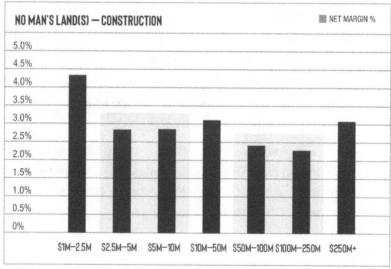

Source: Representative sample of 5.8 million active corporate tax returns filed for 2013.

Key Ideas from Practice 13: Benchmark

- Find out how profitable your company should be by benchmarking it against its industry peers.

- Methodologies include tapping into public IRS databases, consulting your trade association, joining industry peer groups, and applying Mike Michalowicz's Profit First formula.

- Determine where your business is compared to your industry's No Man's Land and use it to decide on major milestones for your business, such as growth, lifestyle business, and exit strategies.

If you would like to benchmark your company and assess your industry's No Man's Land, visit https://BusinessBenchmarker.com.

PRACTICE 14: ENGINEER

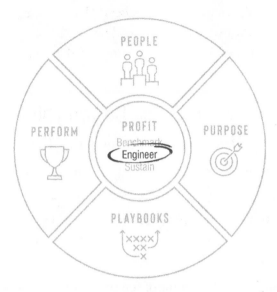

"There are four purposes of improvement: easier, better, faster, and cheaper. These four goals appear in the order of priority."

—Shigeo Shingo

So far, you have benchmarked your business to the top 16 percent of your peers. Now it is time to **Engineer** this business so that you can generate that level of profitability.

If you have implemented the first 13 Pinnacle Practices, there is a good chance that you are already at or near your prescribed profitability level, because you have a business that is aligned with your core values and structured around the right functions, employing all A-Players and A-Potentials, who are being coached to rise to be A-Players themselves.

You have articulated your vision and defined the strategy for how to get there, and your people are aligned with your vision and strategy and are all rowing in the same direction. You are executing your vision and strategy by practicing annual strategic planning and setting quarterly Rocks and weekly metrics for all employees.

Your leadership team and all the leaders below are delegating everything that falls outside their respective unique abilities. They do this with the help of Playbooks that have been defined and ingrained in your organization and are continually being optimized.

How Profitable Do You Think This Business Already Is?

Chances are, it is at an elite level already, but if not, you can do more to make it so.

Let's assume that you have already benchmarked your business against its industry peers and considered the Profit First–suggested Real Revenue margin of 20 percent.

As an example, the top septile of your industry by revenue generates 23 percent net profit. Having implemented the first four Pinnacle Principles of People, Purpose, Playbooks, and Perform, you got to 15 percent net profit. You now have a gap of eight percent profit improvement to make up to be at the elite level.

This gap can be eliminated with one or a combination of the following "low-hanging fruit" approaches, and then continuously improved with a couple of Pinnacle tools, The Power of One, and Love vs. Loath, and finally with the "ultimate approach" we describe at the end of this chapter.

Figure 14.1: Profitability Pine: Ways to engineer higher profit margins

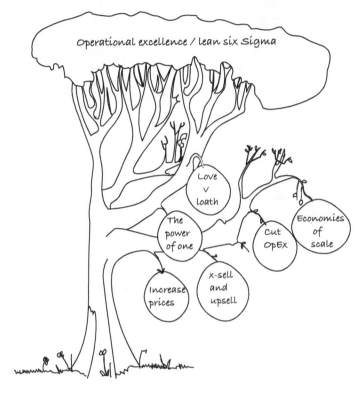

Low-Hanging Approach 1: Increase prices. Unless you are selling a commodity product or service, you may have room to adjust your pricing without significant loss of revenue. Differentiated products and services are often relatively price inelastic.

Necessities such as utilities, prescription drugs, tobacco products, and medical treatments, tend to be inelastic, as are some luxury products, such as iPhones and diamonds. For example, Godaddy.com, the internet domain name registrar and Web hosting company, has increased its domain registration prices dramatically since it was acquired by a consortium of private equity groups in 2011. It's doubtful that they would have done so if it lost them significant sales.

Provided you offer value, a variety of strategies exist for raising prices. Communicate early and make a case for the increase, whether it's supply chain constraints, inflation of inputs, increased value, improvements, or switching to a different service model, such as monthly subscriptions.

You can increase gross margins by bundling products or by creating new tiers at higher prices while offering price-sensitive customers the same price with reduced features.

A client of ours who operates extended-stay hotels for traveling contractors pursued this strategy after upgrading rooms in his hotel. He offered low-budget customers the old prices if they agreed to switch to a container apartment erected on the site, while other customers paid the higher prices for their upgraded accommodations.

If you provide a great and differentiated product or service, most of your happy customers are likely to accept price hikes when you prepare well and communicate the reasons for the change early and openly. No need to apologize for the move, but don't forget to express gratitude for their patronage.

Low-Hanging Approach 2: Cross-sell and upsell other products or services. You can increase your profit margin by coming up with auxiliary solutions and value for your customers.

Happy customers are predisposed to buy from you, and you can solve other problems for them while facing limited competition as an incumbent. If you don't have other products to sell to your customers, partner with companies that have products or services to offer and need your clientele.

Cross-selling and upselling are big business. Amazon reports that it makes up to 35 percent of its revenue this way;[69] that is, it adds an extra 50 cents to every dollar of product sold. What if you, too, could increase your revenues by half with the right offers at the checkout counter? Just ask: "Would you like fries with that?"

So, what's the difference between an upsell and a cross-sell?

- Upselling is offering a better version of the requested model or one with more features at a higher price.

- Cross-selling is selling a related item with the original purchase.

Customers are predisposed to purchasing other offers at the counter because they have already decided to become your customer and you have already broken down the original trust barrier. Further, the incremental cost of the purchase will be compared to a feeling of loss when your customer "deprives themselves" of your enticing upsell offer.

The more products and services you sell to a customer, the more connected they get to your company and will likely stick around longer.

There are proven techniques for effective cross-selling and upselling, such as narrowing choices, offering product bundles, and anchoring the customer's perspective by a dummy offering. Presenting a less attractive alternative to your premium-priced offer will increase the likelihood of acceptance of the upsell option.[70]

Low-Hanging Approach 3: Reduce operating expenses. You may be able to save some costs by relocating your offices to outside of the city or by leasing a smaller space. The latter option is very realistic now that hybrid working has become more prevalent; many employees prefer to work remotely.

You can save payroll expenses by employing people in cheaper geographies inside or outside the United States.

Another option is to build a whole supply chain for your product in Asia, where production is cheaper while quality can be equally high. Tim Cook made his name by building a highly profitable supply chain in China before being promoted to CEO of Apple by Steve Jobs.

Embracing technology is a gamechanger when it comes to reducing operating expenses, especially for digital and service companies. With the explosion of on-demand Software as a Service (SaaS) solutions, technology no longer requires up-front investments and often can be scaled up or down with month-to-month commitment.

This has eliminated the financial barrier to trying new applications. We regularly sign up and experiment with cost-saving technologies even though we know that three out of five services we try would not eventually work out.

The same principle applies to hiring freelancers instead of in-house employees. Millions of solopreneurs offer specialized services on freelancer sites such as Upwork and Reedsy at hourly rates and without any long-term commitment. Just in the past twelve months, we have hired a videographer in Canada, two specialist graphic designers in the UK, a Web developer in Egypt, an e-book programmer in India, a podcast editing firm in the Philippines, and a data analyst in Florida.

Low-Hanging Approach 4: Exploit economies of scale. You may improve your net margin by expanding the business because this allows your overhead to be spread over more revenues. You may also accelerate expansion by acquiring other companies. Synergies often offer cost-reduction opportunities when duplicate functions can be eliminated.

A larger business enjoys higher leverage vis-à-vis suppliers and can negotiate better rates, further increasing margins.

Years ago, Steve worked for a commercial bank that pursued higher profit margins by becoming a one-stop-shop financial services firm. The bank acquired a pension fund, an auto financing business, and a receivable factoring company and launched several start-up businesses, including an asset manager, an equipment leasing firm, and a life insurance business.

By increasing its slate of financial products offered by its network of branches, and by refocusing those outposts to sales by centralizing accounting, data processing, and other support functions, the bank scaled its revenues rapidly.

Other important internal economies of scale include the ability to attract better managers and cheaper insurance because you're perceived as a more stable company. You might even be able to self-insure by absorbing certain risks in-house. A larger company can also attract cheaper debt and capital financing, allowing it to leave smaller competitors in the dust.

An important recent development is the rise of network economies, where the more users a digital platform is able to attract, the more popular it becomes with other potential users and advertisers.

External economies of scale are often created by investments in infrastructure. Silicon Valley emerged in popularity as alumni of early technology companies, most notably Fairchild Semiconductor and later Intel, spurned other entrepreneurial technology ventures. The availability of talent and the energy of innovation attracted other players to the valley and made it the hub for computer companies.

Another external economy is the lobbying power of larger companies, which can influence governmental policies in their favor. Large companies also attract suppliers to their vicinity, creating further advantages.

The Power of One

A powerful Pinnacle tool that helps improve profitability is The Power of One. It is the idea that a mere one percent improvement in each area of your business can easily double or triple your profits. Just growing your revenue by one percent a week would increase your sales by two-thirds in a 12 month period.

But the Power of One is not a purely mathematical formula. Ask every department what they could improve by one percent. Could accounts receivable collect cash one day earlier? Could the construction crew deliver completion one day earlier? Can the sales person convert at one percent better margin? Can the dispatcher get one more item on the schedule? Could the delivery person do one less trip to the job site?

If there was just one thing that we could do a little bit better, faster, more profitably, these changes would compound. At 211 degrees Fahrenheit, we have only hot water, while at 212 degrees we have steam that can power a train. The difference is the power of one.

Love vs. Loath

Another popular Pinnacle tool to use for increasing value and impact is to strike off your to do list everything you hate to do, as you are very likely to not do these things well.

Here is how the tool works: Group all you do into two clusters labelled Love and Loath. Review the Loath list for things you can eliminate, delegate, or automate.

You may think you need that report or meeting, but we challenge you to verify it using the Pareto Principle. Is this item part of the top 20 percent that delivers 80 percent of the value, or it is a bottom 20 percent activity with practically zero value? We all do things that are not worth our time. As Greg likes to say: act your wage!

Creative destruction is a powerful source of profitability and liberation. Years ago, IKEA had a work desk model that Steve bought for everyone on his team at MB Partners. As new people joined the company, they kept buying that desk, until IKEA dropped it from its lineup to improve economies of scale.

Steve was unhappy about the change but soon realized that the other desk model was still the best solution around, even if it did not exactly match the existing fleet of desks.

Can you, too, eliminate some models without a material loss in sales, for a significant growth in profit?

The Ultimate Approach: Drive Operational Excellence

W. Edwards Deming was an American engineer, statistician, and management consultant and one of the catalysts of Japan's industrial revival after World War II. He invented a methodology for continuous improvement called DMAIC (see Figure 14.2), which became a staple tool of the Lean Six Sigma operational improvement movement. (Lean Six Sigma is a method that relies on a collaborative team effort to improve performance by systematically removing waste and reducing variation.)[71]

"DMAIC (pronounced də-MAY-ick) stands for Define, Measure, Analyze, Improve, and Control, and it helps lead a team from defining the problem, through implementing solutions linked to underlying causes, and establishing best practices to make sure the solutions stay in place. DMAIC helps with creative thinking within boundaries, such as when an existing product or service needs to be improved."[72]

Figure 14.2: The DMAIC Process Improvement Model

DEFINE   MEASURE   ANALYZE   IMPROVE   CONTROL

Source: "DMAIC," Wikipedia, last edited February 5, 2022, https://en.wikipedia.org/wiki/DMAIC.

Define: Clearly pronounce the business problem, goal, potential resources, project scope, and high-level project timeline.

Measure: Collect data and establish performance baselines so that improvement can be measured at the end.

Analyze: Identify, validate, and select root causes of waste for elimination.

Improve: Identify creative solutions to eliminate the key root causes, with brainstorming techniques or by conducting experiments.

Control: Embed the changes and make them stick by documenting them as a process or by developing best practices.

If you have already embraced the Pinnacle Principles of People, Purpose, Playbooks and Perform, and harvested the low hanging fruits and Pinnacle tools of cost reduction, and have yet to reach industry-leading profit margins, then focus on improving your operational excellence.

Pick a highly reviewed resource on Lean or Lean Six Sigma to help. *Lean Six Sigma QuickStart Guide: The Simplified Beginner's Guide to Lean Six Sigma* by Benjamin Sweeney is a good place to start.

Key Ideas from Practice 14: Engineer

- Bridge the profit margin gap between your business and the leaders in your industry.

- First exhaust low-hanging approaches such as raising prices, cross-selling and upselling, cutting costs, and harvesting economies of scale.

- Look at each area of your business and apply the Power of One and Love vs. Loath Pinnacle tools to grow the scale and profitability of your business.

- Your final frontier to high profitability is driving operational excellence by applying Lean Six Sigma methodologies.

PRACTICE 15: SUSTAIN

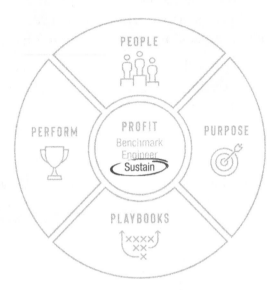

"Success isn't always about greatness. It's about consistency. Consistent hard work leads to success. Greatness will come."

—Dwayne Johnson

Having **Benchmarked** your business against its elite peers and **Engineered** it to be equally profitable, your business has made it to the Pinnacle. Congratulations!

The challenge is to stay there. As successful athletes often say, getting to the top is hard. But staying there is harder.

You can **Sustain** your industry-leading profitability by embracing a handful of strategic concepts that help you stay ahead of competitors, look at the world differently, and keep improving. These concepts are building a Strategy Stack of differentiating activities, Profit/X, and the Flywheel.

Strategy Stack

You can only make your strategic positioning sustainable if you can deliver it with a system of interconnected activities that are different from your competition's. If you are not seen as different, you are actually the same.

A strategy underpinned by a unique collection of activities is hard to copy. In *Great by Choice*[73], Jim Collins calls these the SMaC (Specific, Methodical, and Consistent) Recipe of your business. Verne Harnish calls this stack of approaches "differentiated activities." We call them your Strategy Stack.

Figure 15.1: Your differentiating activities can become your Strategy Stack

Southwest Airlines created the category of the stripped-down budget airline and became the most profitable in its industry. However, few if any competitors were able to achieve similar success because they only selectively copied the Southwest way.

Although most major airlines have since emulated the "no food service" strategy and have squeezed more seats into their planes, most failed to give up interconnecting flights that require baggage transfers. Interlining leads to slower turnaround times at the gates, eroding the margins of these Southwest copycats.

Here are the activities that differentiate Southwest from its competitors:

Southwest Airlines' Strategy Stack

- Boeing 737s only
- 10-minute turns
- No air freight; passengers only
- Frequency of service
- Low fares
- No food service
- No assigned seating
- Batch boarding
- Fringe airports
- Direct routes
- Friendly staff
- Independent sales

IKEA is an industry leader in the furniture sector with a powerful strategy stack. Beyond self-assembly, competitors have to copy a slate of differentiating activities, such as out-of-town locations, attractive designs, and a cost-effective global supply chain, to match IKEA's purchasing power. IKEA's closest competitors, Danish and Austrian copycats JYSK and KIKA, have achieved sales at one-eighth and one-twentieth respectively, of the Swedish giant.

IKEA's Strategy Stack

- Warehouse showrooms
- Easy-to-manufacture designs

- Interchangeable parts

- Global supply chain

- No-air packaging

- Self-assembly

- Winding paths shopping

- Food and child care

- Low prices

Chick-fil-A's differentiators have also blocked successful imitators. The combination of Sundays off, quirky advertising, tasty recipes, a low-cost franchise model, and a unique culture of the place has proved hard to copy.

Chick-fil-A's Strategy Stack

- Closed on Sundays

- Eye contact, smile, and "My pleasure"

- Take orders outside

- Drinks and refills are served at your table

- Order food to your table

- Pickle brine

- Quirky cow ads

- Superior products

- Operator-oriented, low-investment franchise model

- Meticulously cleaned and maintained bathrooms

Chick-fil-A has built a food service chain that has been consistently more profitable than its competitors. The average Chick-fil-A restaurant generated sales of $4.2 million versus $2.7 million for an average McDonald's restaurant.[74,75] Even more impressive, they managed to do that by running corporate-owned stores without needing to tap into the entrepreneurial energy that franchise systems rely on to manage distant employees.

You don't have to be a giant like IKEA or Chick-fil-A to build differentiating activities into your business. Below is a handful of small companies that are doing the same.

Imaging software developer Media Cybernetics:

- Multimodality/file format compatibility

- Consistent user experience in sales and support worldwide

- White-glove, take-care-of-you treatment

- Membership community of passionate users

- Technology-enabling connected laboratory on premises and in the cloud

- Electronic purchase, delivery, and license linking through portal

Business development consultants OST Global Solutions:

- Engage with content

- Bring the right skill mix to solve the problem

- Consult on the full business development life cycle

- Apprenticeship program

- Productized solutions

Distributor of precision measuring equipment

- Personal attention and guidance

- Customer success onboarding process

- Live person answers and calls you back in two hours

- We speak your language

- Pain, challenge, and future state inquiry

- Video training on demand

Fitness franchise Discover Strength

- Personal appearance

- Anticipate and fulfill both spoken and unspoken needs

- Warm welcome and fond farewell while using customer's first name

- Immediate service recovery

- Professional greeting

- Positive language (thank you, certainly, I'd be happy to, etc.)

The beauty of designing and ingraining a string of differentiating activities is that it makes your strategy very difficult to copy. Your competitors would have to imitate all the elements of your strategy to obtain similar results, and even then, you would still continue to enjoy the early-mover advantage in market share and brand recognition.

Profit/X

Jim Collins, in his groundbreaking book *Good to Great,* introduces the "Hedgehog Concept." This model describes the characteristics of businesses that create superior results and can sustain them over a 15 year period.

One of the three elements in the Hedgehog model is what Collins calls the economic engine of the business. This, he argues, can best be measured by a formula named "Profit/X." The X in Profit/X represents a critical constraint in the business that must be leveraged to create value.

If you find a distinctive X for your formula, ahead of your rivals, it can open a "blue ocean" growth opportunity for your business, free of direct competitors.

Southwest Airlines once again is an example. Its formula Profit/Plane (instead of the typical Profit/Seat) allowed it to rethink how to make an airline profitable. It could grow Profit/Plane by working its fleet harder.

Accordingly, the airline picked activities that minimized turnaround times, including building a Boeing 737s–only fleet so that any pilot could be scheduled and eliminating food service and assigned seating.

Starbucks's ratio became Profit/Cup, which led to decisions such as focusing on premium-priced custom drinks, launching a line of "cross-sold-with-coffee" pastries and convenience foods, and adding merchandise sales to their product line.

For examples closer to home, here are the Profit/X formulas some of our private company clients chose:

- Atlas Home Energy Solutions: **Profit/Service Truck** to leverage the most expensive asset used in providing home energy efficiency projects.

- GERSTEL Inc.: **Profit/GERSTEL System**, which focuses on cross-selling services, consumables and high-margin branded accessories.

- Groove Commerce: **Profit/Employee**, points to the need to train employees so that they can provide higher-value expert services over time, and increasing efficiency through automation.

- Media Cybernetics: **Profit/Image Lab**, to center on being a full-service software provider to each penetrated customer in a market with a limited number of targets.

- OST Global Solutions: **Profit/Capture Manager**, to leverage its highly trained and high-salary expert consultants in generating winning proposals for their clients.

Using Profit/X allows you to optimize around your most precious resource. It may be a limited target market, such as the number of image labs for Media Cybernetics, or it may take substantial investment to acquire. AHES spends over $100,000 purchasing and fully outfitting a new truck.

Your biggest opportunity is to develop a formula that is unique in your industry. It allows you to expand with a different strategy from your competitors'. That is what Southwest Airlines achieved with its Profit/Plane metric.

Finding Your Flywheel

In his best-selling monograph, *Turning the Flywheel*, Jim Collins describes a meeting he had with Amazon's top brass in the autumn of 2001. Jeff Bezos had hired him to help the online retailer develop a flywheel concept that would help the leadership think more strategically about engineering a self-sustaining growth momentum in the company.

In *Turning the Flywheel*, Collins argues that sustainable growth is not about achieving a magical breakthrough moment. It is more about pushing a giant flywheel, which would imperceptibly start gaining momentum.[76] "If you work hard for 20 years, you can become an overnight success."

Fortunately, it does not take years to find value in building a flywheel for your business. Creating a flywheel is all about studying which activities make your business gain momentum, and then being intentional about strengthening them.

The Amazon flywheel (Figure 15.2) starts with offering a wide selection and low prices. These attract a growing volume of customer visits, which draws third-party sellers onto the platform. The increased flow of transactions generates the profits that allow Amazon to reinvest in its digital platform and distribution infrastructure. That, in turn, helps grow revenue per fixed costs, allowing the retailer to reduce prices further and expand its selection.

Figure 15.2: The Amazon flywheel

Source: Jim Collins, *Turning the Flywheel.*

Another example is Intel's flywheel: Intel designs new high-powered chips that it can launch at premium prices. (See Figure 15.3.) It then focuses on driving down unit costs to expand the market for the chip and harvests profits even as prices fall. Intel then reinvests its profits in R&D for designing the next generation of microprocessors.

Figure 15.3: The Intel flywheel

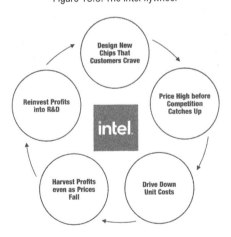

Source: Jim Collins, *Turning the Flywheel.*

As a business owner, you can design your own flywheel. Place your economic engine—we called it Profit/X—at the top of the flywheel so that you are optimizing around your most precious resource. This is a critical part of your growth model.

Then, ponder what will increase your Profit/X. The economic driver at Atlas Home Energy Solutions is Profit/Service Truck. The company can increase that ratio by selling higher-margin products and services.

Next, contemplate what an increased Profit/X ratio will make possible for your company. In AHES's case, it allows the company to invest in training and as a result attract and keep A-Player employees.

After that, you can fill in the remaining cogs in the flywheel. Keep it simple—most flywheels have five to seven cogs total. For AHES, keeping and attracting great people allows the company to deliver innovative, high-quality, customer-focused services, which creates happy recurring and referring customers. (See Figure 15.4.) It is easy to see that this will lead to sales of new and recurring services at increasing margins, spinning AHES's flywheel further.

Figure 15.4: The flywheel of Atlas Home Energy

Source: Courtesy of Atlas Home Energy Solutions.

Check out the other small business flywheels in Figure 15.5. Drivers of small business flywheels may include:

–   Training and attracting great employees

–   Innovating and improving your product (product companies)

–   Increasing customer success

–   Developing new, higher-value offerings (service companies)

–   Creating value-added resources (distributors)

–   Investing in technology

–   Building a community of users

–   Improving sales and marketing

–   Enhancing product delivery

–   Growing existing clients

–   Targeting larger transactions, etc.

Figure 15.5: Other flywheel examples

Source: GERSTEL, Inc.

Source: Discover Strength.

When you have developed your flywheel, ask your team how you can strengthen each cog in the flywheel. Create a list of potential improvements and review them in your quarterly outlook meeting as a fodder for potential Rocks. (See: Practice 10: FAST Rocks chapter earlier in the book.)

Key Ideas from Practice 15: Sustain

- You can sustain high profitability by developing a stack of differentiated activities which, in combination, are hard to copy.

- Find a unique Profit/X denominator that allows your business to swim in a blue ocean, free of direct competition.

- Develop a flywheel for your organization to help intentionally drive the strategic growth momentum of your business.

Messages from Mountain Five: Profit

Build top-tier industry value by Benchmarking and Engineering your profitability to best in class.

Sustaining high profitability depends on developing a stack of differentiated strategies that are difficult for competitors to copy.

Now that you have mastered the Five Pinnacle Principles, it's time to review how your business can ascend to the Pinnacle.

THE CLIMB

"Every mountaintop is within reach if you just keep climbing."

—Barry Finlay

In 1995, the CEO of the formerly state-owned bank OTP had an epiphany. He realized that the bank, which held 60 percent of the deposits of Hungarian savers, was woefully out of touch with modern banking and was rapidly losing ground as international players such as Citibank, Bank Austria, and ABN AMRO entered the market. Other Hungarian banks, such as MKB, were being acquired by western owners as well, who were rapidly modernizing their operations.

Sandor Csanyi, OTP's CEO, responded by hiring the best-renowned and most expensive consulting firm to help him. He retained McKinsey and Company, led by Bulgarian-born, cigar-chewing, bon vivant Anthony Radev to modernize his bank.

McKinsey's consultants moved in and would practically live in the bank for the next decade. By 2002, OTP's stock price had exploded from 790 HUF to over 21,000 HUF, a 26 fold growth. Much of that could be attributed to the systematic approach of transforming a stale bureaucratic institution into a modern, dynamic bank by adopting cutting-edge best practices.

OTP had over 10,000 employees and was a public company when it embarked on its version of the Pinnacle Journey. Your likely much smaller private company may not be able to invest in McKinsey's services, but you do have the option of applying a management blueprint yourself or hiring a guide to help you get to the top of your business mountain.

This is exactly what Luke Carlson, the CEO of Minneapolis-based fitness company Discover Strength, did when he hired Greg in 2014. Luke had started the business eight years earlier and had been an avid reader of all the business classics, including *The E-Myth*, all of Jim Collins's works, *Scaling Up*, and *Traction*, but could not institutionalize the principles in his own business.

Most other fitness companies saw themselves as lifestyle businesses or at best real estate companies, but Luke wanted to have it both ways: build a purpose-driven organization that can also make money.

"As with most 'all-knowing' CEOs, I felt uncomfortable bringing in an outside guide to tell me what to do. However, I was stuck and needed help and decided to bite the bullet."

In the next eight years Discover Strength grew its revenue 10-times from $700,000 to over $7 million and 10X'd its profit margin to 16 percent, which is at the elite level in his industry.

Discover Strength has grown from a single location into a fully differentiated, thriving, national franchise brand, where staff turnover is virtually zero. The value of the business grew by at least 250 times of what it was in 2014.

"It was the best business decision we've ever made," said Luke. "Greg allowed me to not have to facilitate but actually participate in our offsite meetings. Our summits are the highlights of each quarter, where we close the period behind us and reset and get pumped up for the quarter ahead."

In this section of the book, we will review some of the management blueprints available to you as a shortcut to orchestrating your business into a self-managing, fast-growing, and highly profitable entity. We will also discuss the pros and cons of hiring a guide to help you climb your business mountain.

MANAGEMENT BLUEPRINTS

"It is the mark of an educated mind to be able to entertain a thought without accepting it."

—Aristotle

In his previous book, *Buyable: Your Guide to Building a Self-Managing, Fast-Growing, and High-Profit Business*, Steve talks about Seven Management Concepts that companies on the Fortune 1000 have all implemented with the help of business school graduates.

Your challenge is that your private business may not be big enough to carry the salaries of Harvard and Stanford MBAs to do the same for you. Even if you were willing to invest a king's ransom, these high-flyers might still probably choose to work for larger companies, where they could move up the career ladder and make more money faster.

Here is where the concept of "management blueprints," also often called "business operating systems," comes in. These are business recipe books that help smaller private companies implement the management and strategy concepts and tools that their public and *Fortune*-listed counterparts have been using for decades. (See Figure 16.1.)

The Blueprint Revolution started with the 1976 publication of Michael Gerber's *The E-Myth*, which he reissued as a business fable 10 years later under the title *The E-Myth Revisited*.

In this seminal book, Gerber explains the entrepreneurial myth, which is that entrepreneurs start businesses. He makes the case that most businesses are actually launched by subject matter experts he calls "technicians" who just want to be their own bosses or who have just lost their job and are forced to work for themselves to put food on the table.

The E-Myth teaches these technicians how to think like managers and entrepreneurs by explaining how to define business functions, practice strategic planning, and document processes.

The next management blueprint book that came out was Jack Stack's *The Great Game of Business* in 1991, the story of which we shared in Practice 11: Metrics.

Figure 16.1: The six most popular Management Blueprints

Jack Stack opened up his company's books to his employees and insisted on using a scoreboard to stay on track with quarterly plans. This was a set of weekly metrics that allowed employees to focus on actionable activities and helped them be more focused and impactful.

It took another 11 years for the third recipe book to be published. It was Verne Harnish's *Mastering the Rockefeller Habits*. Harnish had founded the Entrepreneurs Organization in the early 1990s and chaired its Birthing of Giants Program at MIT. Participants included such legendary entrepreneurs as Steve Jobs, Michael Dell, and Mark Cuban.

Harnish's innovation was to turn concepts into "tools," making his framework more tangible and easier to implement.

His tools included the One Page Strategic Plan (actually on two sides of one page), which operated as a simplified business plan. It displayed the core values, purpose, vision, certain elements of strategy, and the annual and quarterly plans of the organization. He also created a forty-point questionnaire to help you improve your business.

The next book was *Traction: Get a Grip on Your Business* by Gino Wickman in 2007. Wickman was the day-to-day manager of a sales training company founded by his father. The Wickmans hired a Verne Harnish coach to advise them, and after their family business was sold, Gino joined Verne's company, Gazelles, as an implementer of the Gazelles management system.

Gino later left and simplified some of Verne's concepts and created tools of his own. He called it Virtual CEO, and later the Entrepreneurial Operating System (EOS). Over time, he refined EOS and started hiring other implementers as licensees to teach the system.

EOS grew, and by the mid-2010s had become the most popular system, with over two hundred accredited implementer licensees.

Having witnessed the success of EOS and building on two decades of experience with Gazelles, Verne Harnish returned with *Scaling Up: Rockefeller Habits 2.0* in 2014. By that time, the Gazelles organization had rebranded as Scaling Up and targeted fast-growing businesses with excellent new tools such as the Talent Assessment, the 7 Strata of Strategy, and the Strengths, Weakness, Trends (SWT) sheet.

Scaling Up was followed by *The 4 Disciplines of Execution (4DX)* from the pen of Sean Covey (son of Stephen Covey, author of *7 Habits of Highly Effective People*), Chris McChesney, and Jim Hulli.

4DX put the spotlight on setting a powerful Big Hairy Audacious Goal, which they called the Wildly Important Goal, breaking it down to annual and quarterly objectives, and measuring employees with custom metrics reflecting individual contributions.

The authors emphasized that the challenge of successful execution is to generate lasting behavioral change in executives and employees alike.

Treating *Rockefeller Habits* and *Scaling Up* as two versions of the same system, these are the five most important business operating systems in use. (To learn more about these and five other blueprints, read Chapter 5 of *Buyable*.)

Which management blueprint is the right one for you?

If you answered, "all of them," then you are on the right path. You don't *have to* pick a business operating system the same way that you don't have to choose a cancer treatment. After all, how would you decide between radiation therapy, chemotherapy, and surgery—by conducting Google search? We bet you would rather visit the Mayo Clinic and pick a doctor who will select the right treatment for you.

We are solving three problems for entrepreneurs and their leadership teams:

1. Which Business Operating Systems should you choose? Which is the right one for you?

2. Once you choose the system, where and how do you find an experienced person to help you customize and personalize the system for your unique company?

3. No one single Business Operating System has *all* the answers, yet you need a complete and comprehensive business operating system with no weak areas or gaps. Remember your system is perfectly designed to give you the results you are getting. If the business operating system has gaps or weaknesses, it will limit your growth.

Who Is the Right Guide for You?

Although you will probably benefit from the services of any experienced guide, finding one who is the right fit will make your journey much more rewarding.

Pick a guide you have good chemistry with, one who has been where you want to go, and who is curious to learn about your people and your business. Pick the guide who is willing to rope in with you and make sure that you and your team members find their way to the Pinnacle and return to base camp alive.

We have realized over the years that we resonate with certain types of clients more than with others. The most important is the character and motivations of the primary decision maker that we are supporting. Is that person in it just to cash some checks and is willing to sacrifice their team to get there? Or are they motivated by a desire to help others and make a difference? The Pinnacle System is all about building, equipping, and empowering a team that will climb together to reach worthwhile peaks.

What kind of guide would you like? Would you want someone who is willing to enter the danger and push you to grow, or you prefer someone who will please you by reflecting your own opinions.

It helps if the guide is intrigued by your business, because this motivates them to figure out how to help you build the right team and the right strategy. Pick a guide who is passionate about what you do, whether it is services, manufacturing, technology, distribution, or professional advice, etc. Experience in your field and curiosity about your niche are good signs that you are talking with the right person.

On the other hand, the guide is not there to be an industry expert. Greg was auditioning for a dermatology practice that was interviewing people to help them implement a business operating system. Toward the end of the audition, one of the owner-doctors had a conversation with Greg:

"Greg, what do you know about dermatology?"

"I know very little about dermatology, but let me ask you a question: Did you invite me here today because you don't know enough of dermatology, or you need help with culture, people, process, and performance?"

"The latter."

"Then I can help you. I know a lot about these."

Greg was subsequently chosen and worked with the dermatology practice for several years.

Finally, you want to work with someone you like, who shares your values, and exudes the right energy. Your guide will be there to build trust and engage and inspire your team. Pick someone with the personality and credibility that will help you survive and thrive through the inevitable challenges of the journey ahead.

Thankfully we have a fast-growing community of seasoned guides to choose from across North America and overseas. They have all run companies for themselves or others and have likely trodden the paths that you are about to embark on. Learn more about them at https://PinnacleBusinessGuides.com.

Self-Guiding the Climb

If you have gotten this far in this book, chances are you have already decided to apply at least some of the ideas and concepts we've talked about.

Eighty percent of the readers of such books as this will try to implement what they have learned themselves. If you are a small company with limited resources, you may feel that you cannot afford to hire a guide. Or perhaps you just don't like to involve outsiders in your business and prefer to implement what you learn by yourself.

Both of these approaches are understandable, and Steve can relate to them, because he did the same in his time after reading *The E-Myth* and *Traction*.

If this is the case, then you can follow the chapters as they are laid out in this book. We recommend that you study the books we mentioned along the way; you can consult the Endnotes for a complete list of titles.

The very basics of the Pinnacle system is a structured strategic planning model that breaks down your vision into a strategy and plan and execution tools to monitor their accomplishments. Again, the best way to visualize it is with the Pinnacle Pyramid.

The Pinnacle Pyramid

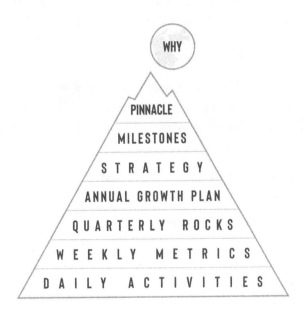

In hindsight, Steve wishes he had someone guide him when implementing the *E-Myth* and *Traction* systems. Beyond reading about Michael Gerber's services, which felt out of reach at the time, he was unaware of any guides in Europe who helped small companies implement business blueprints. Even if he had been aware, Steve might not have used them, assuming he could do these things himself.

When we look back on our career as business guides, we see that our respective learning curves have been steep, and they still are. We cannot imagine why our clients tolerated our inexperience in the early days—they probably did not know any better.

Implementing a customized business operating system requires an understanding of the context of the journey and how the different climbing tools relate to the skills and personality makeup of each leadership team. It is easy to be overwhelmed, and it takes experience to find the goldilocks zone, where the learning is energizing and creates enthusiasm for the implementation. Going slow bores people, and moving fast burns them out.

We can go as fast as you and the team can go. If you have a young, fit, small team, we can sprint to the first summit. If the team is large, unhealthy, and no longer fired up to take the hill in a larger business, it's going to take more time to get to the first summit.

Luke Carlson of Discover Strength believes that investing in a guide makes his company take the climb much more seriously and their financial commitment forces his team to prepare thoroughly ahead of summits to make sure they get a great return on their money.

If you still prefer to try to self-implement, here is Steve's seven-step advice:

1. Read this book three more times and study all the other books we mention in this volume. Immerse yourself in the sciences of entrepreneurship, management, and leadership and develop curiosity and passion for the subject.

2. Consider finding two to three smaller companies that can't afford a guide and offer to teach them Pinnacle tools for practice.

3. After starting to work with your own team, be and appear to be objective without seeking a specific outcome. Do that even if the result changes the mission that you had written for your company's website.

4. Ask for complete openness from your leadership team and commit to and demonstrate that you will not punish them for any dissenting opinions. The Pinnacle system involves leadership disciplines that

have to be co-discovered and co-created by your team so that everyone contributes to and becomes part of the process.

5. Hold yourself and everyone else in the company accountable. Be ready to walk the talk and try to do each piece of the process to close to 100 percent while celebrating everyone else when they approach 80 percent.

6. If anyone of your team is confused or pushes back on any piece of the system, have an explanation, analogy, or a story at hand to clarify it for them.

7. Join a peer group of other leaders who are self-implementing Pinnacle, so that you can bounce ideas off them whenever you are stuck.

These are the steps Steve recommends you take to self-guide your Pinnacle climb, but Greg is skeptical whether it can even be done. This is not a journey for the faint of heart. It takes time, a financial investment, and perseverance to climb to the top. That is why few make it there.

Also, most accidents happen with climbers on the way down. Not every business owner is able to orchestrate a well arranged and timely exit or transition. All of us will hand over our keys at some point—hopefully to someone eager to take it for a large sum of money. But many entrepreneurs transition without anyone showing up to pick up their keys.

Now there you have it.

If you would like to discuss your specific situation with an experienced Pinnacle Business Guide and explore what the journey could be like with or without one, visit https://PinnacleBusinessGuides.com.

CLIMBING TOOLS

"If someone tells you that you have enough climbing gear and you don't need any more, you should stop talking to them. You don't need that kind of negativity in your life."

—Rachel Peterson

Bedrock Tools

The Pinnacle philosophy is to be system agnostic. No author has cornered the market for good ideas, and we want to stand on the shoulders of all those creative individuals who have come before us.

The bedrock tools of Pinnacle are taught during Base Camp, and they are the Strategic Vision and Execution Plan (SVEP), Talent Assessment, Strategy Squares, Meeting Structures, Win the Week, FAST Rock Planner, and the Employee and Client Journey Playbooks.

With the help of these seven bedrock tools, you will:

1. Discover the core values that drive your business and who should be climbing with you.

2. Plan who should be doing what, who should report to whom, and what "good" looks like.

3. Learn who your A-Players are, whom you should protect and promote, and learn who are your A-Potentials, whom you should be coaching to become A-Players.

4. Articulate the vision for your business and your strategy to get there.

5. Build a strategic plan for the next three to five years.

6. Master a cadence of execution of these plans with quarterly, monthly, and weekly touchpoints of accountability.

7. Design Your most important Playbooks for your Customer and Employee Journeys, respectively.

Let's review each basic tool in turn.

Strategic Vision and Execution Plan

The underlying idea of the SVEP is to summarize the elements of the culture, vision, strategy, and annual and quarterly plans of the company. Reviewing this simple tool quarterly with your people reinforces alignment across the company.

Figure 17.1: Strategic Vision and Execution Plan (SVEP)

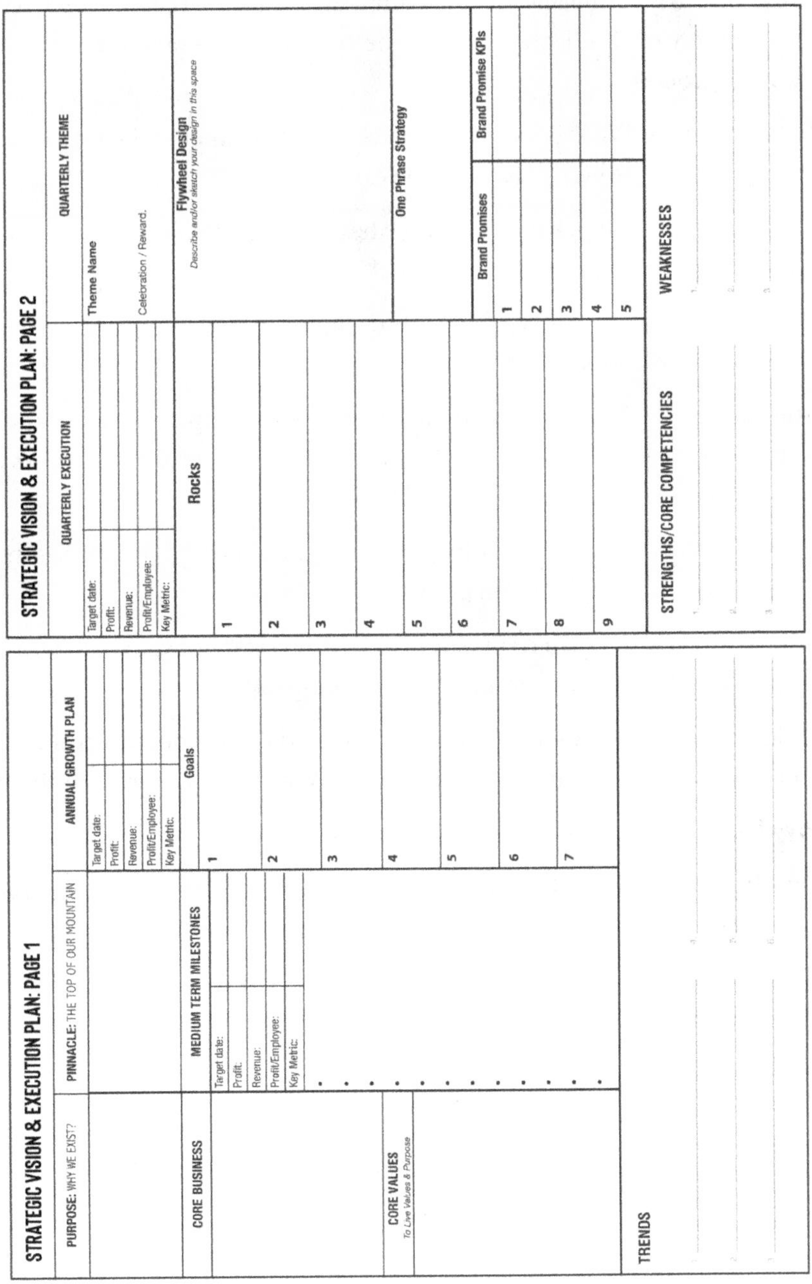

STRATEGIC VISION & EXECUTION PLAN: PAGE 1

PURPOSE: WHY WE EXIST?

PINNACLE: THE TOP OF OUR MOUNTAIN

ANNUAL GROWTH PLAN

Target date:
Profit:
Revenue:
Profit/Employee:
Key Metric:

CORE BUSINESS

MEDIUM TERM MILESTONES

Target date:
Profit:
Revenue:
Profit/Employee:
Key Metric:

Goals

1
2
3
4
5
6
7

CORE VALUES
To Live Values & Purpose

TRENDS

STRATEGIC VISION & EXECUTION PLAN: PAGE 2

QUARTERLY EXECUTION

QUARTERLY THEME

Theme Name

Celebration / Reward.

Target date:
Profit:
Revenue:
Profit/Employee:
Key Metric:

Rocks

1
2
3
4
5
6
7
8
9

Flywheel Design
Describe and/or sketch your design in this space

One Phrase Strategy

Brand Promises	Brand Promise KPIs
1	
2	
3	
4	
5	

STRENGTHS/CORE COMPETENCIES

WEAKNESSES

The elements of the SVEP are the following:

Why. How is your business contributing to others? How do you aspire to change the world in a way that can be true for 100 years, even as your business evolves?

Core Business. What is the sweet spot business segment where you have the potential to be better than anyone else?

Core Values. What behaviors do your best people exhibit that have made you successful as a company?

Pinnacle. What is your Big Hairy Audacious Goal, the Pinnacle of your mountain, 7 to 20 years from now?

Medium-term Milestones. What does your company look like in technicolor three years from now? What are the broad-brush milestones to be achieved while getting there?

Annual Growth Plan. What are your key financial targets and the handful of initiatives that will help you grow this year?

Trends. What changes in technology, product, market, consumer, and social attitudes could impact your industry and company?

Quarterly FAST Rocks and Theme. What are the priorities that will move you closer to your annual goals this quarter? What is this quarter all about?

Flywheel. What does your flywheel look like? How can you spin it faster?

One-Phrase Strategy. How can you express your strategy in a simple phrase so that everyone in your company can put it into action?

Brand Promises and KPIs. What three to five things does your brand stand for? What are your Kept Promise Indicators (KPIs) to prove it?

Strengths/Core Competencies. What can you do better than others in the eyes of your target customers?

Weaknesses. What weaknesses do you have that aren't likely to change?

Topics. What are the topics you need to tackle in your next quarterly summit to move the company forward?

By understanding and internalizing your SVEP, your employees will have a crystal-clear vision of how your company can succeed. The SVEP will help them make daily decisions to move your business forward.

Function Ownership Chart

The Function Ownership Chart is a tool that was originally developed by Michael Gerber in *The E-Myth*. He called the main functions "positions" and the list of related outcomes a "Position Contract" between the business and the employee. Verne Harnish and Gino Wickman refined these concepts and called them "functions" and "roles," Respectively.

We call these Functions and Outcomes because what we care about for each Function is to deliver the Outcomes the company is counting on. We discussed the Function Ownership Chart and the accompanying the Win-the-Week Scoreboard, in detail in Practice 2: Functions.

Figure 17.2: Two-level Function Ownership Chart

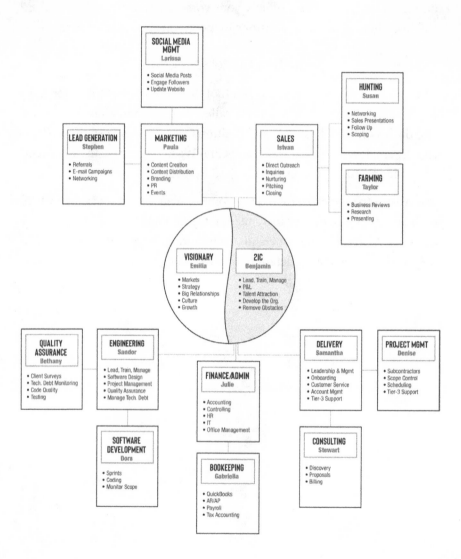

The goal is to define the organization that will take your business to the next level over the next six to twelve months. What are the functions and the outcomes you need to deliver on? Who are the people best able to execute on these? Let's put the right people in the right seats.

Win-the-Week Scoreboard

So far, you have defined the Functions and Outcomes your organization needs to grow to the next level. You have also found the best person in the organization to take charge of each Function. In smaller organizations, a handful of key people including the owner will likely be heading multiple Functions. Your goal is to decide which ones to delegate first going forward, so that everyone can focus on high value-add activities.

You have created your Function Ownership Chart. But how do you know whether your Function Owners are executing and delivering on the outcomes they own?

Enter the Win-the-Week Scoreboard.

Jack Stack articulated the need to create a weekly scoreboard for your company that tracks real-time results. Verne Harnish thought that you should develop one or two daily or weekly measurables for each of your employees so that they know how to be successful and contribute to achieving the company's goals.

In the Pinnacle system, we use a gamified "Win-the-Week Scoreboard," which gives you a reason to celebrate each week won and each quarter in which a majority of the weeks have been won. (See Figure 17.1.)

What are the most important outcomes your function owners must deliver on? What does a great week look like for these outcomes?

In the example below, Emilia's highest-value contribution as a Visionary is to enhance the audience and market share of the business by building important relationships with key clients and strategic partners. She is also in charge of spreading the message of the company by giving talks and interviews and writing blog posts.

Benjamin, as the 2IC, is in charge of running day-to-day operations. His key Outcomes are generating the profit and cash flow targets laid down in the business plan so that the company can keep growing. He has a competent C-level team, and his main job is to coach and mentor his A-Player and A-Potential direct reports so that they deliver a great job in their respective functions.

Benjamin's, other metric measures the number of conversations he has with prospective hires he wants to attract to the organization. He is all about building and improving the team.

Paula in marketing is focusing on generating leads and improving brand awareness by creating valuable content and engaging prospects on social media. Istvan in sales is focusing on issuing relevant proposals that convert leads into monthly recurring revenue (MRR) clients.

Sandor in engineering does a great job if new releases are launched on time and users are happy. His metrics are open tickets and the managing of technical debt so that the software is fast and bug free.

Figure 17.3: Win the Week Scoreboard (see an enlarged version on page: 44)

FUNCTION	OWNER	OUTCOMES	METRICS	TARGET/WEEK	RESULTS	METER	WON?
VISIONARY	Emilia	# of followers Market share Market cap	# of big relationships touched # of talks, interviews, blogs	3 2	4 1		Y N
2IC	Benjamin	Profit Cash flow	# of coaching conversations # of talent prospect conversations	5 2	5 3		Y Y
MARKETING	Paula	Lead flow Social media engagement Brand awareness	# of qualified leads # of content pieces distributed	4 3	2 3		N Y
SALES	Istvan	Sales revenue New logos acquired	# of proposals issued $ of new MRR contracted	3 $5,000	2 $5,500		N Y
ENGINEERING	Sandor	Regular new releases Happy users	# of open tickets Staff utilization %	<=5 80%	2.5% 75%		Y N
DELIVERY	Samantha	Gross profit Growing existing customers	# of hours billed # of business reviews	600 2	625 0		Y N
FINANCE/ADMIN	Julie	Quickbooks is accurate & up to date Helpful and updated Scoreboards	$ of invoices issued Receivable days	$160,000 30	$180,000 42		Y Y
WON THE WEEK?							9/5

Talent Assessment

Having defined your company's core values and having put the right people in the right functions, it is time to assess your talent pool. Who are your A-Players and A-Potentials? Are you allowing your time to be drained in conversations with B- or C-Players instead of mentoring A-Potentials and finding bigger jobs for A-Players?

Are there any C-Players in your company? It's time to do the right thing for the company and for the C-Player, who needs a new challenge and the opportunity to start over in a more suitable job.

Use the Talent Assessment tool (Figure 17.2), courtesy of Verne Harnish, who created this tool for *Scaling Up*. Have each of your leaders prepare their coaching and action plans for their direct reports.

Figure 17.4: Talent Assessment tool, Part 1

TEAM MEMBER INITIALS	CULTURAL FIT SCORE 0-10	PRODUCTIVITY SCORE 0-10	RATING: A. B. B/C. C	ACTION /COACHING PLAN

Source: Verne Harnish, Scaling Up

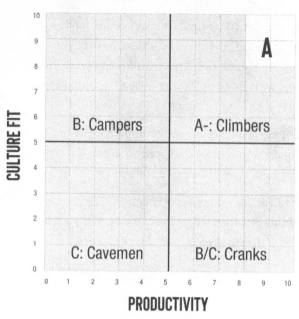

Figure 17.5: Talent Assessment tool - Part 2

Source: Verne Harnish, Scaling Up

Strategy Squares

After nailing down your core values, the Why, the Pinnacle, and the Medium-term Milestones for your company, the Strategy Squares tool helps you position and differentiate your business.

The economic landscape is littered with businesses that make commodity products and provide generic services. If you don't stand out as different, the market will want you to be the lowest-priced solution, and you will be hard pressed to make a profit or have quality, paying customers.

Figure 17.6: Strategy Squares

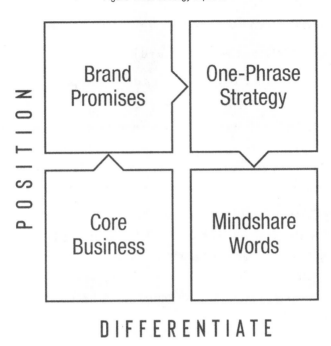

Meeting Structures

In his book *Death by Meeting,* Patrick Lencioni talks about the different meetings companies *should* be using to communicate, solve problems, create structured accountability, and align the organization around their vision, strategy, and plan.

The essential meetings are the Daily Standup, Weekly Tactical, Monthly Financial and Rock Review, and five full-day strategy sessions a year, including three Quarterly Lookouts and a two-day Annual Summit. (See Figure 40.)

Each of these meetings have different objectives and agendas:

Daily Standup. This is a daily meeting to exchange critical information and focus the team on the tasks of the day ahead. In five to fifteen minutes, team members answer three questions:

1. What happened yesterday that the team needs to know?

2. What will happen today that the team needs to know?

3. Where am I stuck or where do I need help?

The goal of this meeting is to create a daily touchpoint and to eliminate inefficient ad hoc meetings that tend to leave some people out of the loop.

Weekly Tactical. This meeting is held on a regular day and at a regular time. The tactical meeting is designed to review the progress of the week, including metrics, Rocks, customers, employees, and business development and to identify topics to be discussed and actioned.

Monthly Financial and Rock Review. This is a two- to four-hour meeting designed to stay on track with quarterly financial targets and Rocks. The leadership team compares actual versus budget figures line by line on the income statement and the cash flow report. Rocks are examined in detail, and the team decides how to get off-track items back on track in the coming weeks.

Figure 17.7: Essential Meeting Structures

ANNUAL	Planning
QUARTERLY	Strategic
QUARTERLY	All-hands
MONTHLY	Financial
WEEKLY	Tactical
DAILY	Standup

Source: Adapted from Patrick Lencioni, *Death by Meeting* (Jossey-Bass, 2004).

Quarterly Lookouts. The leadership team meets quarterly to review financial results and Rock completion and to align around the vision, the strategy, and the plan, which is refined if necessary. After diagnosing priority topics, your Pinnacle Business Guide may bring one or two new climbing tools for the team to implement before setting financial plans and Rocks and selecting a theme for the next quarter. The back side of the meeting is spent working on the list of topics, creating action items for the team, and improving team health.

Annual Summit. This is a two-day offsite meeting where the team evaluates the past 12 months and creates a new strategic plan for the coming year. The summit includes reviewing trends, strategizing, improving the vision to ensure it remains fresh and exciting, and working on the trust and openness of the team.

The two days culminate with the creation of a new Annual Growth Plan, with themes that can be socialized well across the company, to propel forward momentum.

FAST Rock Planner

Following quarterly and annual meetings, each member of the leadership team creates project plans for any Rocks they own with the help of a FAST Rock Planner worksheet.

FAST stands for Frequently reviewed, Ambitious, Specific, and Transparent, to emphasize that Rocks need to be widely shared across the company and must push the envelope, not sandbag. The FAST Rock Planner is designed to highlight and mitigate any obstacles to Rock completion such as dependencies on outside vendors and other departments.

Figure 17.8: FAST Rock Planner

F.A.S.T. ROCK PLANNER

ROCK OWNER:		DUE DATE:

ROCK TITLE:

DESCRIBE THE ROCK AND IS IT FAST?

Why is this ROCK important?

ROCK STEPS

BY DATE	ACTIVITY FOR ACHIEVING THE ROCK	
	First Step [+]	
	Mid Step [+]	
	Mid Step [+]	
	Mid Step [+]	
	Final Step [+]	

LIST RESOURCES NEEDED FOR COMPLETION

Customer and Employee Journey Playbooks

No business can be scaled without Playbooks, and it's best to start with your Customer Journey Playbook, that helps you attract and grow paying customers, the lifeblood of your business.

Your next Playbook should most likely be your Employee Journey Playbook, so that you can attract A-Players and A-Potentials for your business and make sure they are indoctrinated in your culture and are happy and productive. Hiring is the new "sales", and it is even more challenging than that for many companies in the post-pandemic age.

Figure: 17.9: Employee Journey Playbook Template

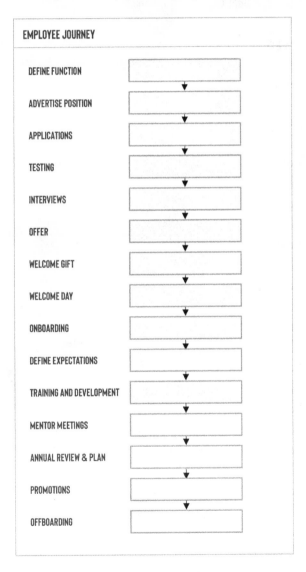

Source: Inspired by David Jenyn's: Systemology

Figure: 17.10: Customer Journey Playbook Template

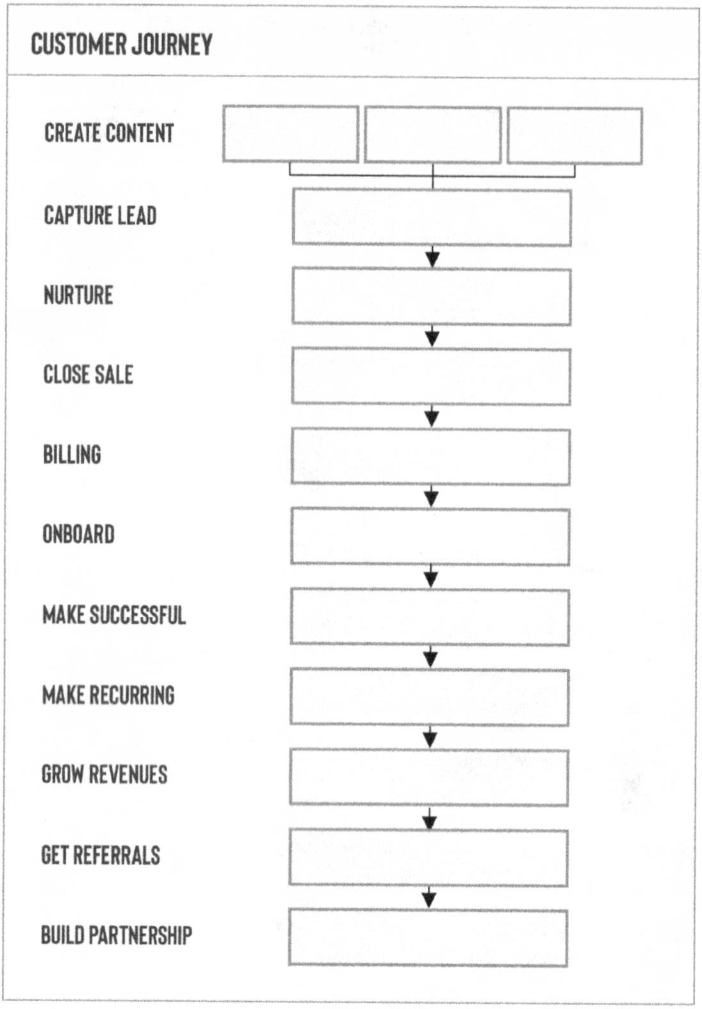

CUSTOMER JOURNEY

CREATE CONTENT	☐ ☐ ☐
CAPTURE LEAD	☐
NURTURE	☐
CLOSE SALE	☐
BILLING	☐
ONBOARD	☐
MAKE SUCCESSFUL	☐
MAKE RECURRING	☐
GROW REVENUES	☐
GET REFERRALS	☐
BUILD PARTNERSHIP	☐

Source: Inspired by David Jenyn's Systemology

Higher-Level Pinnacle Tools

The idea behind the Pinnacle Journey is for it to be a fully customized management blueprint for growing companies. After introducing the basic toolkit to your company, your chosen guide is responsible for customizing the program for your team by bringing you the right tool at the right time.

The Pinnacle Business Guides organization employs a "tool cabinet," a committee of volunteer guides who develop new tools for the Pinnacle Guide community every calendar quarter. The tool cabinet already contains more than 60 tools, most of which aren't implemented for years, until the time that your company needs them.

Messages from The Climb

Management blueprints help you conceptualize and implement practical tools that shortcut company growth. But they are not for everyone—you need a team that genuinely wants to grow and is willing to open their books and be vulnerable with each other.

Selecting the right guide for your company's climb can be lifesaving and create a faster and smoother route to the Pinnacle. Start the climb by focusing on implementing the basic tools of the Pinnacle system. Once you master the basic climbing tools, a Pinnacle Business Guide can help you find the right advanced growth tools and keep you ascending ever upward.

You can choose to track your progress and manage your Pinnacle tools in a purpose-designed software application such as the Pinnacle App[77] or the Rubicon Software for Pinnacle.[78]

Now that you know what it takes to climb your business mountain, read on to find out what it feels like to reach the Pinnacle.

THE PINNACLE

"Any time you finish a climb,
there's always the next thing you can try."

—Alex Honnold

A little over two decades ago, Steve and a good friend, Beco, decided to go
back to Greece, where they had spent a memorable month backpacking and
island-hopping with two other friends while at college.

One afternoon, they decided to climb the highest point on the island.
There were six peaks in the Psiloritis mountain range, and they picked the
one that appeared to be the highest. After driving their rental car to the
highest point possible, they began climbing the enormous pile of rocks to
the top.

It was a grueling climb without proper gear. The sun bore down on them, and gusts of wind nearly blew them off the mountain. Only their egos kept them from turning back. They had to conquer Crete!

Imagine their disappointment when, after finally reaching the top, they realized a yet higher peak soared beyond the valley... Steve and Beco encountered what is called a "false peak."

Setting out to reach the Pinnacle of *your* business may become a similar experience. As soon as you reach it, you might see a bigger and more exciting Pinnacle beyond it. This will be your time to descend and start climbing again—or to hand over your climbing tools to a next generation of leaders.

Your Pinnacle Journey

So, what does it take to get your business to the Pinnacle?

The first step is to upgrade your team to the point where all of your **People** are A-Players or A-Potentials who exhibit your **Culture** (core values) and consistently perform at a high level.

Then you need to define your Function Ownership Chart and list the outcomes required for each **Function** to take your business to the next level over the following six to twelve months. Put A-Players and A-Potentials in those functions.

Implement a process for **Coaching** your A-Potentials by using the Socratic method so that *they* learn to be self-reliant and come up with their own solutions. Ensure that you and your team are having Mentor Meetings each quarter with your respective direct reports to give and receive feedback, clarify mutual expectations and re-energize the relationship.

To pursue your business **Purpose**, gather your leadership team and articulate your company's **Vision**, including the Why of your organization and its long-term audacious goal called the Pinnacle. Paint the Medium-term Milestones of your business, including key financial targets and the broad-brush, high-level achievements you are striving to accomplish along the way.

Define your core business and the ideal customers that you are pursuing and develop a differentiated **Strategy** of achieving your vision, including brand promises with kept promise indicators (KPIs) proving that you are delivering on them. Synthesize your strategy into a single phrase that allows everyone in your company to understand it and execute on it.

Achieve the **Alignment** of your team around your vision and strategy by regularly reinforcing your Strategic Vision and Execution Plan with them and by integrating your core values and strategy into every facet of your business.

At the end of each year, take your leadership team offsite for a two-day annual summit to update and recommit to your vision and strategy and to review your Medium-term Milestones and formulate a new Annual Growth Plan.

Strive to **Perform** at a high level and accomplish your Annual Growth Plan by breaking it down into quarterly plans, setting FAST **Rocks,** and adjusting your weekly **Metrics.** Make sure you gamify your scoreboards and challenge your teams to win the week and win the quarter.

Review these metrics in weekly tactical and monthly financial and Rock review **Meetings,** and work with your leadership team to keep each other on track with achieving them.

Along the way, **Define** the core processes of your business and document **Playbooks** for them. Assign owners to each playbook and task them to **Ingrain** them into your organization with the ultimate goal to eliminate single person dependency in your business.

Over time, **Optimize** your Playbooks by analyzing them to find and then remove bottlenecks, roadblocks, and waste. Simplify them by eliminating these obstacles and by automating processes wherever possible. Consider embracing technology to liberate your staff from the burden of repetitive tasks.

Having climbed the first four mountains your business should be churning out high **Profits** already. This is the time to **Benchmark** your profitability to the elite of your industry. When you know the gap to cover between where you are and where you want to be, it is time to **Engineer** your business to generate the profits you want and deserve. **Sustaining** that level of profitability will require you to build a differentiated Strategy Stack, to ward off copycat competitors.

Extending the Climb

A group of clients started to climb their mountains with Steve in 2017 by implementing a management blueprint called the Entrepreneurial Operating System (EOS). They had great success with that system, but about two years in, Steve started running out of material to teach them.

Meetings became repetitive, and Steve wondered how he could develop a next-level toolbox for these clients. He wanted to fill some gaps with more strategy tools, introduce additional exercises to improve their team cohesion, and teach concepts to develop their people further. This dilemma wasn't EOS-specific; it would have arisen with other closed-end management blueprints as well.

Then, in early 2021, Steve learned about Pinnacle Business Guides, founded by Greg, a community of former EOS Implementers and guides who had transitioned from other systems.

The open architecture of the Pinnacle management blueprint concept has revolutionized the thinking of the business guides in our community. It opened the door to creating custom operating systems for our clients by immersing ourselves in their specific challenges and constructing unique journeys tailored to them.

Beyond the basic execution tools of visions, annual plans, Rocks, Metrics, and Meetings, each client is on a different climb and faces unique challenges. Our job as guides is to meet them where they are and bring them the right business tool that addresses their most burning needs.

Elevating Founders

Along the climb to the Pinnacle, a breakthrough moment arises when a founder finally let's go, takes the leap, and empowers their team.

In late 2018 after two years of flat organizational growth, eCommerce agency Groove Commerce set a 10 year goal of having a company with one hundred employees in the right seats. Soon after, the CEO promoted one of his associates to a 2IC role to take charge of coordinating activities at the leadership level.

After three years following this process, the company tripled its revenue and is on course to meet its Pinnacle—three years early! Soon they will have to come up with a bigger Pinnacle to keep the journey exciting for the team.

Another one of our clients, the Reichle Klein Group (RKG), a commercial real estate company, set out to become a $4 million property management company by 2030. Around the time they embarked on the climb to this Pinnacle, the founder hired an operation-minded executive and over the following years gradually delegated all critical functions of the operations of that business and elevated him to the 2IC role.

As a result, RKG is already halfway toward its goal, with a chance of getting there within the next one or two years. It will be time for them, too, to find the next Pinnacle soon.

In both cases, the journey to the Pinnacle accelerated as the leadership team relieved the founder of overseeing day-to-day activities. The move was catalyzed by first creating organizational clarity, structured accountability, and systemizing the business, which enabled the leadership team to delegate tactical execution.

The Decision

So, what are you going to do? Are you ready to clarify your Why and set a Pinnacle for your business? Having a great purpose and a big, audacious, long-term goal can turn your quest into an exciting adventure that will inspire you and your people and attract A-Player candidates to your business.

Your decision is whether to change or stay with the status quo. The Pinnacle is waiting for you.

Messages from the Pinnacle

Getting your business to the Pinnacle is highly satisfying and will likely help you bring the next Pinnacle into view. You may actually start to see separate Pinnacles for your business and your personal life.

By following the five Pinnacle Principles and the underlying 15 Pinnacle Practices, you will turn your business into a category of one in your industry, with an elite group of A-Players and industry-leading profitability.

At some point, your personal journey may diverge from that of your company's, but your business's Pinnacle journey can become infinite, with your company scaling increasing heights over time.

Are you ready to take the first step to leading your team to the top?

CONCLUSION

"All you've got to do is decide and the hardest part is over."

—Tony Wheeler

Steve's journey of discovering management blueprints started with Michael Gerber's *E-Myth* and Gino Wickman's *Traction*. Each of these books transformed his business, and over time led to discovering dozens of other blueprints. You can read about 10 of these in *Buyable: Your Guide the Building a Self-Managing, Fast-Growing, and High-Profit Business* and by listening to Steve discuss scores more with entrepreneurs, who use them, on the *Management Blueprint* podcast.

We love management blueprints because they help you apply complex management and business-building principles in synthesized form. Paraphrasing Orit Gadiesh and James Gilbert from the *HBR* monograph, *On Strategy*: a management concept that is 80 percent accurate that people understand well enough to apply is better than a 100 percent accurate concept that overwhelms you.

Today, we stand on the shoulders of entrepreneurial giants. As the owner of an emerging private business, you now have the opportunity to apply in practical form a wealth of research and theories developed by such eminent thinkers as Frederick W. Taylor, Peter Drucker, Jim Collins, Michael Gerber, Michael Porter, Jack Stack, Verne Harnish, Gino Wickman, Patrick Lencioni, David Jenyns, and others.

Pinnacle is the "Linux of business operating systems": it is an architecture that applies practicable business concepts and translates and teaches them to entrepreneurial leadership teams. Our community of Pinnacle Business Guides wants you and your leadership team to easily grasp and apply the essence of these concepts in your business, starting today.

With the five Pinnacle Principles—People, Purpose, Playbooks, Perform, and Profit—and the fifteen Pinnacle Practices described in this book, you can transform your business, no matter where you're starting out on your mountain climb. Give it a couple of years, and you will have turned a stumbling business into a good one or an already good business into a great one.

You can shortcut your path to the Pinnacle by picking a business guide who has already been where you are going. Your guide will meet you where you are at, teach you the basic climbing tools, and curate higher-level tools for you, as and when you need them.

When you arrive at the Pinnacle and enjoy the 360-degree view from there, you can then decide whether to keep your business climbing to a new, higher Pinnacle or start a new climb toward your own personal ideal life.

The Pinnacle Journey begins with a simple step. Make a decision to begin, and start applying the Pinnacle Principles and Practices today.

REVIEW REQUEST

Thanks for reading! If you enjoyed this book or found it useful, we'd be grateful if you'd post a short review on Amazon. Your support really does make a difference, and because we will read all the reviews, we'll be able to get your feedback and make this book even better for a possible future edition.

Thanks again for your support!

Steve Preda and Gregory Cleary

ACKNOWLEDGMENTS

The biggest inspiration for this book was my co-author, Greg Cleary, the creator of the Pinnacle Principles, and the mastermind of the idea of creating an open source and scalable business operating system.

I feel gratitude to my immediate family, including my wife, Dora, and my children, Emilia, Paula, Istvan, and Sandor, who cheerled the process and tended to my support during the endless hours of writing and editing.

Greg is grateful to his family; Julie, his soul mate; and his children Samantha and Benjamin, who bring the inspiration to get up each day and figure out how to be a better father, husband, friend, and guide.

My longtime friend and personal coach, Dave Quick, encouraged me to pen the book and helped to brainstorm chapters that were not fully formed in my mind. So did Arvin Delgado, who spurred me in between our tennis games whenever my enthusiasm started to flag.

Greg and I are standing on the shoulders of giants, including Peter Drucker, Andy Grove, Michael Gerber, Jack Stack, Jim Collins, Verne Harnish, Gino Wickman, Simon Sinek, David Jenyns, and other authors who have come before us and laid the groundwork by creating business frameworks, concepts, and operating systems that inspired Pinnacle.

Our editors, Christina Palaia and copyeditor and proofreader Nicole Hall, and Barry Lyons helped us refine the narrative and avoid grammatical and stylistic landmines, while our graphic designers, Jason Anscomb, Zoltan Ember, Greg Kimmes, Will Sargent, and Andy Meaden helped create an amazing cover and internal design. I hope you the reader like it too. We also owe special thanks to Toni Culley for creating an accurate and handy Index.

Along the way, a group of amazing Pinnacle Guides provided ideas and inspiration, including: Duane Marshall, Michael Erath, Richard Palmer-Smith, Rebecca Lockwood, George Hodges-Fulton, Jeff Tritt, John Fulwider, Jon O'Malley, Jeff Chastain, Jason Rothfuss, Daniel Magill, Connie Chwan,

Cullen Talley, Dan Sedor, Deb Thompson, Forth Heffner, Jim Palzewicz, Keith Trost, Linda Ratner, Mark Rockwell, Paul Tetrault, Preston True, Rick Appleby, Rick Drumm, Tom Barrett, Todd Hanson, Kyle Breischaft, Megan Alarid, John Gaudet, Doug Hall, Ryan Giles, Scott Elser, Barbara Foulkrod, Ben Stewart, Doug Tenpas, Mark Rockwell and Tip Quilter, and many more.

My amazing Vistage chair friends, including Debbie Tyler, Clyde Northrop, David Daugherty, Wally Schmader, Brian Roberts, Mike Tubridy, Amy Gleklen, Tom Parker, Matt Lauth, and others allowed me to try out some of the ideas in front of their business-leader peer groups and encouraged their members to listen with an open mind and give valuable feedback that helped shape nascent tools. My own Vistage group alumni, such as Matt Williams, Jeri Turley, Rob White, Jeff Marks, and Brian Burnette, gave their critiques and helped chisel some early concepts into productive Pinnacle tools.

Members of my circle in Richmond and Budapest, including Mike Metzger, Nasser Chanda, Glenn Kurtz, and Natalie Garramone, have also given invaluable feedback during the writing process, as did Andras Scharle, Zsolt Rieder, Adam Zatik, and Lajos Vargedo. Bennet Coles and Richard Kelly mentored me along the way.

Last but not least, we are grateful to our clients who agreed to share their stories on these pages, including: Matt Sera, Vikram Raya, Ravi Gupta, Lenny Giller, Michael Yudovin, Ethan Giffin, Adam Luecking, Harlan Reichle, Olessia Smotrova, Dave Huff, Christopher Brement, Joe Mallek, Stephen and David Ogburn, Steve Deller, Bob Collins, Heinan Landa, Nick Beavers, Chandresh Trivedi, Luke Carlson, Stefan Freeman, Michael Comstock, Kevin Koppang, Randy Shie, Kurt Plechaty, Jaime Gmach, Harry Brown Family, Kristi Piehl, Kevin Falconer, Bruce Soma, Todd McVay, Jonathan & David Dworsky, Tony Fiorillo, Steven Ayres, Mike Crippen, Greg Elliott, Jill Blashack Strahan, Brandon Mensink, Patrick Murphy, Mike Smith, Dan Fagan, and Jon Ryan.

Thank you!
Steve and Greg

ABOUT THE AUTHORS

STEVE PREDA is a Leadership Team Coach whose passion is to help privately owned businesses grow and thrive. He pursues it by simplifying and teaching management and strategy concepts used by large companies and elite consulting firms.

Since 2012, he has helped over 100 businesses grow their teams, revenues, and profits as a business coach, EOS Implementer, and as a Pinnacle Business Guide.

Steve explores business-growth shortcuts on the Management Blueprint podcast, and delivers workshops and keynotes to business leaders around the US. He loves helping growth-minded entrepreneurs and their leadership teams reach their business-pinnacles.

GREGORY CLEARY is a Leadership Team Coach, and the Founder of Pinnacle Business Guides.

Greg began his career with Brian Tracy at Peak Performers. Over the years, he has worked with such legends as Jim Rohn, Og Mandino, Tom Hopkins, and many others.

Greg was one of the first EOS Implementers, and he implemented EOS with 149 companies before founding Pinnacle Business Guides. Today Greg helps the Pinnacle Business Guide community of guides to take their clients to the summit of their mountains... while actually enjoying their climbs.

FURTHER RESOURCES

Author's Home Page — Steve Preda: https://StevePreda.com
Author's Home Page — Gregory Cleary: https://GregoryCleary.com
Pinnacle Business Guides Directory: https://PinnacleBusinessGuides.com

Steve Preda: *Buyable: How to Build a Self-Managing, Fast-Growing and High-Profit Business* (Glen Allen, Amershire Publishing, 2021)

Buyability Assessment: https://BuyabilityAssessment.com

Management Blueprint Podcast: https://bit.ly/MBPpodcast
Succession Secrets Podcast: https://apple.co/39RBsah

ENDNOTES

1 https://www.youtube.com/watch?v=81Ub0SMxZQo

2 Michael Gerber, *The E-Myth: Why Most Small Businesses Don't Work and What to Do About It* (New York: Harper & Row, 1986)

3 Jim Collins: *Good to Great: Why Some Companies Make the Leap... and Others Don't* (HarperBusiness, New York, 2001)

4 https://www.jimcollins.com/article_topics/articles/first-who.html

5 Jim C. Collins and William C. Lazier, *Beyond Entrepreneurship: Turning Your Business into an Enduring Great Company* (New York, Prentice Hall Press, 1995)

6 https://www.sba.gov/sites/default/files/Business-Survival.pdf

7 https://www.jimcollins.com/pdf/Mars_Group.pdf

8 https://hbr.org/2002/07/make-your-values-mean-something?cm_sp=Article-_-Links-_-Comment

9 Steve Preda, *Buyable: How to Build a Self-Managing, Fast-Growing and High-Profit Business* (Glen Allen, Amershire Publishing, 2021)

10 Framework coined by Pinnacle Business Guide, Keith Trost.

11 Gino Wickman, *Traction: Get a Grip on Your Business* (Dallas, Benbella Books, 2011)

12 https://www.amazon.com/Unique-Ability-Creating-Life-Want/dp/1896635628/

13 The Pareto principle: https://en.wikipedia.org/wiki/Pareto_principle

14 Susan Scott, *Fierce Conversations: Achieving Success at Work &in Life One Conversation at a Time* (New York, Berkley Books, 2004)

15 Napoleon Hill, *Think and Grow Rich*, (Meridien, CT, The Ralston Society, 1937)

16 Jim Collins, Jerry Porras, *Built to Last: Successful Habits of Visionary Companies* (New York, Harper Business, 1994)

17 Simon Sinek: Start with Why https://www.youtube.com/watch?v=u4ZoJKF_VuA&vl=en

18 Tesla's Why: https://www.tesla.com/about

19 https://www.patagonia.com.au/pages/our-mission

20 https://www.walgreensbootsalliance.com/

21 https://www.businessinsider.com/elon-musk-mars-colonies-human-survival-2015-10

22 https://mission-statement.com/general-motors/

23 https://www.oprah.com/pressroom/oprah-and-discovery-communications-announce-own-the-oprah-w/all

24 https://futurism.com/tesla-aims-to-be-a-one-stop-shop-for-all-of-your-sustainable-energy-needs

25 https://www.forbes.com/sites/bizcarson/2019/06/06/23andme-dna-test-anne-wojcicki-prevention-plans-drug-development/?sh=67f43245494

26 https://traveltomorrow.com/elon-musks-starship-fully-reusable-rocket-to-revolutionise-space-travel/

27 https://ebonylifefilms.com/ebonylife-media/

28 https://drivenxdesign.com/now/project.asp?ID=17912

29 Verne Harnish, *Scaling Up: How a Few Companies Make It… and the Rest Don't* (Miami, Gazelles, Inc., 2014)

30 HBR's 10 Must Reads on Strategy 2-Volume Collection (Harvard Business Review Press, Boston, MA, 2020)

31 https://www.dsbcreative.co/article/three-key-elements-to-a-killer-brand-promise

32 https://www.23andme.com/dna-health-ancestry/

33 https://www.forbes.com/sites/forbesbusinesscouncil/2021/03/26/how-to-develop-and-keep-your-service-promise/?sh=10ec8be86051

34 http://www.bmwstyle.tv/the-ultimate-driving-campaign/

35 https://www.patagonia.com/core-values/

36 https://www.actonegovernment.com/talentmanagement.aspx

37 *Transforming Corner-Office Strategy into Frontline Action* by Orit Gadiesh and James L. Gilbert, (Harvard Business Review, May 2001). https://hbr.org/2001/05/transforming-corner-office-strategy-into-frontline-action

38 https://www.fastcompany.com/3057837/the-man-behind-ikeas-world-conquering-flat-pack-design

39 https://www.fastcompany.com/887990/starbucks-third-place-and-creating-ultimate-customer-experience

40 https://www.tableau.com/solutions/customer/southwest-airlines-maintains-time-flights-and-optimizes-fleet-performance-tableau

41 Based on approximately 115,000 commercial flights per day reported by FlightRadar24: https://www.flightradar24.com/data/statistics and approximately 25,500 commercial aircraft in the world according tom Statista.com: https://www.statista.com/statistics/282237/aircraft-fleet-size/

42 https://www.investopedia.com/terms/j/jack-welch.asp

43 Jim Collins and Jerry I. Porras: *Built to Last: Successful Habits of Visionary Companies* (HarperCollins, New York, 1994 p202-203)

44 https://chickfilapodcast.com/why-does-chick-fil-a-say-my-pleasure/

45 https://en.wikipedia.org/wiki/Pareto_principle

46 David Jenyns: SYSTEMology: Create Time, Reduce Errors and Scale Your Profits with Proven Business Systems (SYSTEMology, Prahran, Australia, 2020)

47 Thepinnacle.app

48 Nawras Skhmot, "The 8 Wastes of Lean," The Lean Way, August 5, 2017, https://theleanway.net/The-8-Wastes-of-Lean.

49 *Intelligent Automation: Learn how to harness Artificial Intelligence to boost business & make our world more human* (Self-published, San Francisco, 2020)

50 https://www.techtarget.com/searchenterpriseai/definition/machine-learning-ML

51 https://www.mckinsey.com/~/media/mckinsey/business%20functions/mckinsey%20digital/our%20insights/intelligent%20process%20automation%20the%20engine%20at%20the%20core%20of%20the%20next%20generation%20operating%20model/intelligent-process-automation.pdf?shouldIndex=false

52 Richard borrowed (and further evolved) the concept from Dan Wallace, Co-founder of The Traction Group. https://www.linkedin.com/in/danwallace1/

53 Endnote appears as a footnote on page 129.

54 Donald Sull and Charles Sull: *With Goals, FAST Beats SMART* (MITSloan Management Review, 2018) https://mitsmr.com/2M0tVWe

55 Based on the concept elaborated by Mike Michalowitz in his book with the same title.

56 As told by Jim Collins in his book *Good to Great*.

57 https://www.facebook.com/OfficialJimRohn/posts/some-things-you-have-to-do-every-day-eating-seven-apples-on-saturday-night-inste/10151153690835635/

58 Source of example: Richard Palmer-Smith, Pinnacle Business Guide, Boulder, CO

59 Patrick Lencioni: *Death by Meeting: A Leadership Fable...About Solving the Most Painful Problem in Business* (Jossey-Bass, San Francisco, CA, 2004)

60 https://en.wikipedia.org/wiki/OODA_loop

61 Patrick Lencioni: *Five Dysfunctions of a Team: A Leadership Fable* (Jossey-Bass, San Francisco, CA, 2002)

62 https://gpsforsmallbusiness.com/talking-about-people-issues-dont-know-how/

63 https://theconversation.com/how-spacex-lowered-costs-and-reduced-barriers-to-space-112586

64 https://www.torquenews.com/14335/teslas-staggering-battery-advantage-over-its-competitors

65 The Pareto principle states that approximately 20 percent of most populations represent 80 percent of the value. Steve managed to determine the expected value of the top and bottom 16 percent of the populations, representing approximately 2 standard deviations from the mean.

66 Philip Wilson: *2016 Almanac of Business and Industrial Financial ratios* (Walters Kluwer, Chicago, 2015)

67 https://www.irs.gov/statistics/soi-tax-stats-corporation-source-book-data-file

68 Doug Tatum, *No Man's Land* (Portfolio, 2008).

69 https://www.wtmdigital.com/blog/ecommerce-upselling-and-cross-selling/

70 https://theconversation.com/the-decoy-effect-how-you-are-influenced-to-choose-without-really-knowing-it-111259

71 "Lean Six Sigma," Wikipedia, last edited January 10, 2022, https://en.wikipedia.org/wiki/Lean_Six_Sigma.

72 Michael L. George, David Rowlands, Mark Price, and John Maxey, *The Lean Six Sigma Pocket Toolbook: A Quick Reference Guide to 100 Tools for Improving Quality and Speed* (McGraw-Hill, 2004).

73 Jim Collins and Morten T. Hansen: *Great by Choice: Uncertainty, Chaos, and Luck - Why some thrive despite them all* (HarperCollins, New York, 2011)

74 Alex Lockie, "How Profitable Is Owning a McDonald's Franchise?" 1851, March 19, 2021, https://1851franchise.com/how-profitable-is-owning-a-mcdonalds-franchise-2715302.

75 Kate Taylor, "Chick-fil-A Is the Fast-Food Chain of the Year, and Things Are Only Getting Better," Business Insider, December 28, 2018, https://www.businessinsider.com/chick-fil-a-is-the-fast-food-chain-of-2018-2018-12.

76 Jim Collins: *Turning the Flywheel: A Monograph to Accompany Good to Great* (Harper Business, New York, NY, 2019)

77 https://www.thepinnacle.app

78 https://www.PinnacleRubicon.com

INDEX

transparent, 20-21, 229
tree method of decision making, 49, 53
Trends, 220
trunk decision, 49
trust deficit, 158
Turning the Flywheel (Collins), 196
Twenty Groups, 172
23andMe, 63, 71

U

Unique Ability, 39-40
upsell, 182-183
Upwork.com, 44, 184

V

value engineering, 164
value traps, 30-32
venture-funded, 19
Veravas, 60, 64
Virtual CEO, 209
Vision, 57-66, 77-82, 87
        How, 58-60
        long-term goal, 57
        What, 62-64
        Why, 57-62
visionary company, 82
Visionary, 38-39, 108-109
Vistage, 167

W

WAIT, 157
Walgreens Boots Alliance, 59
Waste, 121-122
Weaknesses, 220
weekly metrics, 42, 144-145, 237
weekly tactical, 51, 111, 139, 153-154, 228
        financial performance, 154
Welch, Jack, 74
Why, 82, 87, 131, 220
        Atlas Home Energy, 83-85
        Media Cybernetics, 85
Wickman, Gino, 38, 209, 221
Win-the Week Scoreboard, 42-43, 147-148,
        217-218, 223-224
workflow automation, 123-124
workflow management tools, 125

Z

Zapier, 124
Ziglar, Zig, 23

CPSIA information can be obtained
at www.ICGtesting.com
Printed in the USA
LVHW111422230522
719440LV00034B/33/J